INSTRUCTIONAL

COACHING

CONNECTION

BUILDING RELATIONSHIPS TO
BETTER SUPPORT TEACHERS

DR. NATHAN LANG-RAAD

Instructional Coaching Connection: Building Relationships to Better Support Teachers
©2022 Nathan D. Lang-Raad

This book is available at special discounts when purchased in quantity for educational purposes or for use as premiums, promotions, or fundraisers. For inquiries and details, contact the publisher at books@daveburgessconsulting.com.

Published by Dave Burgess Consulting, Inc.
San Diego, CA
DaveBurgessConsulting.com
Library of Congress Control Number: 2022931461
Paperback ISBN: 978-1-956306-15-6
Ebook ISBN: 978-1-956306-16-3

Cover and interior design by Liz Schreiter
Edited and produced by Reading List Editorial
ReadingListEditorial.com

To all you educators.

Your students' lives are forever changed because you believe in them and work so relentlessly for them.

CONTENTS

FOREWORD

BY JIM KNIGHT

In the spring of 2016, a threat to my health shook my world. I was in Connecticut, collaborating with a great group of educators, who generously invited me out to dinner. As I answered emails, waiting for them to finish up their after-school meeting, I suddenly felt the whole left side of my body go numb. When I stood up, I struggled to walk. I ended up in the local hospital, and after many tests and after the symptoms stopped, I was diagnosed with a chronic migraine and released.

My life partner, Jenny, flew out to meet me and fly home with me. While I felt fine at first, as our flight continued, I began to feel worse. At first, I couldn't read the words on my computer screen. Then, I struggled to talk. By the time Jenny took me to our local hospital, I couldn't say the simplest of words, and I was experiencing an impossibly painful headache. The pain was so intense and my confusion was so overwhelming that I thought I might be dying. I told Jenny that if this was it, she really should remarry.

Well, I didn't die. I was just experiencing a second, more intense round of symptoms of the chronic migraine. Thankfully, I've never experienced those symptoms again. I share this story because when I really started to wonder if my life might be over, and when I had to ask myself, "Has this been enough?" the only thing I thought about were my relationships—my connection with my spouse, my kids, my grandkids, my friends, all the people I know, and how imperfectly I had connected with others. Relationships, for me, are everything.

This is why I am so grateful for Dr. Nathan Lang-Raad's beautifully written book about coaching. The book is built around the pillars of empowered, effective relationships at work and in our lives. In wise and accessible ways, Nathan writes about fundamentally important topics, such as the power of purpose; the importance of establishing rapport, being visible to each other, balancing collaboration and independence; the necessity of listening, empathy, and communication. What especially impresses me is that throughout this book, Nathan's important ideas are simply and beautifully stated. Nathan's voice embodies the respectful, warm, supportive approach he proposes for coaching conversations.

Over the years, many, many coaches have told me that one of the wonderful benefits of being a coach is that the skills of coaching are the skills of life. Indeed, and as I like to say, coaching is life. This book will help you be much more effective as a coach. More importantly, it will help you become a better person—a person who has better relationships. And when the time comes to take stock of your life, I believe you'll find that those relationships really matter.

INTRODUCTION

Take a moment and think about what prompted you to take the leap into an instructional coaching role. What made you make the move to stop teaching kids and start mentoring, supporting, and coaching adults? That's quite a significant shift, isn't it? It's one that the majority of teachers don't want to make, but you did. Why?

I'm deeply passionate about coaching. It's hard work, but it's one of the most fulfilling things I've ever been a part of. It may sound selfish, but I love the feeling I get when I watch someone I've been coaching do things they never thought they could or would do. When I witness them step out of their comfort zone, learn and grow, stretch themselves, take risks, take pride in an accomplishment, and make changes that amplify the learning of their students, I can't help but love this work, and I consider it a gift. I take that seriously, and I never want to waste it. I don't think there is another environment where exceptional coaching is more influential or essential than it is in our schools and classrooms. We have such a tremendous responsibility to educate our children and to help them realize their full potential. Educators make a difference at the generational level.

For me, the move into a supportive-leadership role came quicker than I had initially intended. I was twenty-seven years old when I was appointed my first leadership role as an assistant principal. I had been a high school science teacher, and before that, I had worked at NASA as an education supervisor. I'd also worked as a high school administrator, adjunct professor, and as the director of curriculum and instruction for elementary schools in a large urban district (87,000 students), where I had the opportunity to work alongside over one hundred instructional coaches. Then, an opportunity presented itself to me: to help lead a school to become a science, technology, engineering, and math (STEM) magnet school, focused on project-based learning and collaborative teacher planning.

I was excited to use my experiences in the classroom and at NASA to support teachers and students in this new endeavor, we had a humongous task ahead of us: to adopt a brand-new set of standards, implement a new teacher-evaluation system, create all-new scope and sequences, and implement a new state assessment for students. All of this needed to be tackled in the first year! It was a busy but amazing adventure, and we couldn't have experienced the success we experienced had we not created a collaborative and productive community of instructional coaches and teacher-leaders. I learned so much about coaching from watching superior coaches in action, and they inspired me to write my first book about instructional coaching, *Everyday Instructional Coaching: Seven Daily Drivers to Increase Teacher Effectiveness.*

In every role I've had, my favorite part was the relational aspect: Who was this colleague? Why did they get into education? What can I learn from this person? What characteristics make this person a great teacher? How can I best illuminate their talents and skills? How can I best support this person and partner alongside them? The relational and connective aspects of coaching led me to consider similar models for relating information, which brought me to neuroscience. When scientists needed a word for the map of connections in the human brain, they created a portmanteau, starting from the term *genome* used in DNA research, which refers to all the genetic material of an organism—in other words, the totality of an organism's DNA. In order to express the totality of the brain's pathways and connections, neuroscientists coined the word *connectome*. Like the genome, the connectome is a comprehensive diagram of neural connections in the brain.

Everything in a brain, all the memories, personalities, skills, fears, etc., are located somewhere within the map of those neural connections. Scientists are currently mapping all of the neural connections within an organism's nervous system—the connectome—through the work of the Human Connectome Project at the National Institutes of Health.

That struck me, because connection is the true essence of coaching. A coaching connectome—a map of the pathways necessary for effective instructional coaching—could provide a really useful perspective on this work. When educators think about a school, they probably think about a complex machine with "many moving pieces and parts," as many colloquially say in the school world. It's natural to compare this with the brain and its many neural connections. Each neural pathway has a specific job and role, but taken collectively, the whole system works like a processor. Likewise, the idea of a "coaching connection" can serve as an instructional coaching map for the school setting. In this analogy, the coach is a central processor, and their experiences, decisions, behaviors, and interactions flow along certain pathways to educators. These pathways all have distinct functions while retaining their connective nature. The goal of the coaching connection is to help coaches learn to use these pathways to best support the teachers they partner with.

In this book, I will focus on six pathways: sincerity, confidence, culture, communication, emotional intelligence, and leadership.

PATHWAY OF SINCERITY

Coaches have a deep passion, not only for the practice of teaching but, more importantly, for the practice of supporting teachers. The biggest challenge instructional coaches face in this work is in creating, building, and maintaining relationships. They must not only be able to work alongside a teacher and win their trust, but they also need to do so with sincerity and genuine intention. Even with this important priority, moving down the path, with its obstacles and relational challenges, can make coaches feel like they're isolated and on their own. Often, coaches and teachers encounter resistance, mistrust, and hurt feelings while pursuing collaboration for growth. What we know for certain is simple: the foundations of building authentic relationships are good communication and sincere intention.

PATHWAY OF CONFIDENCE

What makes coaches effective in navigating school culture? Developing the strength to accept their own idiosyncrasies can help coaches boost confidence in their skills and experiences. They can examine their thoughts, opinions, and feelings without worrying about popularity. They can speak clearly and confidently because they have developed a rich sense of self. A characteristic of confident communicators is that they love themselves well enough to believe they are worthy of kindness and compassion from others without exception. And this confidence can be passed along to teachers. When turbulence threatens to pull them off the path while they're interacting with others, coaches can react with patience, confidence, and positive intention.

PATHWAY OF CULTURE

A healthy school culture built around rapport promotes the sharing of concerns and fears, as well as unbridled celebration. If, as a leader and a coach, you don't hear concerns, you should be concerned. It is a privilege to be the recipient of a concern. It means that the person across from you, looking you in the eye, trusts you enough to think you should hear and understand their perspective. Never underestimate this kind of gift. In a world that is sometimes inured to truth, do not forget to honor the plain honesty of one moment of mutual understanding.

PATHWAY OF COMMUNICATION

Coaches have wellsprings of strategies, advice, concepts, and ideas, but none of it matters without an effective communication pathway. Being an effective communicator hinges entirely upon being a good listener and being able to ask good questions. Good listeners are unfazed, patient, and immune to the chaos that might be caused in their minds by the actions of others. They have the capacity to not be rattled or descend into defensiveness, even when they hear information that challenges their deeply held assumptions. Effective communicators use their experience, and they draw on moments when they've overcome challenges to build a reserve of equanimity within themselves. They will have the composure to recognize, defuse, and navigate potentially bewildering situations.

PATHWAY OF EMOTIONAL INTELLIGENCE

Real and lasting change is a result of the everyday actions of the teacher in the classroom—and the everyday support teachers receive from the instructional coach. Some days it feels like our purpose has wandered from the path, and we forget the destination we are moving toward. School-wide transformation is not only an all-hands-on-deck effort but a decision for each individual to do their own reflective work. This requires patience with ourselves and emotional maturity. Emotional maturity begins with the strength to sense and admit without defensiveness our own infantile, irrational, or impulsive behaviors. If we are truly being self-aware, we are regularly embarrassed by our actions, we laugh at ourselves, and then we grow from the insight we gain about ourselves.

PATHWAY OF LEADERSHIP

Well-functioning coaching systems require effective leadership structures that empower teachers. Changing traditional practices, expectations, and guiding principles requires calculated risks, input, order, strategic decision-making, and a clear and courageous vision. A pathway of leadership focuses on the creation of an instructional coaching framework that supports all stakeholders and develops a cohesive plan for coaches who are supporting teachers.

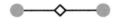

The pathways in the brain are composed of nerve cells, which transmit impulses across a synapse. Synapses are like essential bridges allowing information to move from one place to another. As a part of the network-connection map I am proposing here, the term *synapse* will be used to describe actions I suggest for coaches, so that they can best support teachers. Synapses are opportunities to put ideas, goals, and strategies into action. Think of the synapses as coaching challenges.

As you explore each pathway in the instructional coaching connection, I want to challenge you to think about how each pathway serves a distinct purpose and how it is connected to the larger network of pathways. As coaches, we don't act in isolation. Our behaviors aren't one-off decisions based on external stimuli. Our vision drives our goals, and our goals help to establish the outcomes we want to accomplish. The pathways help to connect our vision, our goals, and our outcomes in meaningful ways so that we're able to make better decisions with confidence while seeing how those decisions impact other aspects of the world—school, classrooms, team meetings, and more—around us.

PATHWAY OF SINCERITY

HOW DO YOU APPROACH COACHING?

The coach must approach the coach-teacher relationship from a position and posture of sincerity. Sincerity is the mechanism by which one person feels they can relate to another. Sincerity boosts connection, first by providing a sense of equity—"we are on the same playing field, neither of us is better than the other, we are both flawed human beings, etc." Sincerity also implies a sense of truthfulness—that is, a sense that you can believe and trust in what you're being told.

In order to begin improving a sense of sincerity, coaches need to be clear on what their role is and what it isn't. Even though coaching has been around for a couple of decades, I recognize that in some respects the instructional coaching role is still being defined, and what is expected of coaches tends to vary from system to system. I thought it might be important to share with you my definition of coaching— what I believe it is and what I believe it isn't—as we begin mapping out the coaching connection. Throughout this book, we'll dive deeper into what it takes to be a successful coach who ultimately impacts student learning, but I wanted to share a few initial thoughts to kick us off because ambiguity leads to coaches spending their days doing everything else but what they were hired to do: coach. Sincerity cannot fully take hold in the coach-teacher relationship in the presence of ambiguity.

The role of an instructional coach should be to partner directly with teachers with a common goal of improving the quality of instruction in order to have a positive impact on student learning.

The role of an instructional coach should be to partner directly with teachers with a common goal of improving the quality of instruction in order to have a positive impact on student learning.

◆ **WHAT COACHING ISN'T:**

- Test coordination
- "Fixing" teachers
- Critical and judgmental
- Directive and evaluative
- An opportunity for a go-to substitute or quick fill-in teacher
- "Friendship" with teachers
- School-wide interventions
- Thinking everyone should teach like you taught
- Simply providing people with materials and resources

◆ **WHAT COACHING IS:**

- **Collaborative:** Coaching is a partnership between the coach and the teacher focused on maximizing student learning through high-quality instruction.

- **Individualized:** Coaching isn't about making all teachers the same or comparing one to another. It's about appreciating each person for who they are and what they bring to the table and supporting them on their unique journeys to grow as practitioners.
- **Purposeful and detail oriented:** Coaching is planning for the many strategic everyday decisions that connect with your intrinsic purpose.
- **Grounded in learning:** Coaching is ensuring we are growing teacher practice so that students can learn at the highest levels.
- **Open and responsive:** Coaching is a delicate balance between two oscillating needs—decisiveness to ensure the work gets done and, at the same time, a great openness to new ideas.
- **Focused and well planned:** Coaching is about creating structures to ensure that there is a consistent rhythm for the everyday moments and provide an anchor of stability during uncertain times.
- **Systematic:** Coaching is interconnected. One component affects another. All the dominoes on the board must be considered.
- **Complex:** Coaching is highly complex because humans are complex. Recognizing this complexity is an opportunity to be our most authentic selves.

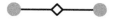

It's important that you determine what your beliefs (beliefs beget sincerity) are about coaching and what beliefs lead to productive work and what beliefs lead to unproductive work.

Use this table to list those beliefs. I have filled in a few rows with examples to get you started:

IDENTIFYING BELIEFS ABOUT COACHING	
Unproductive Coaching	**Productive Coaching**
The role of the coach is to tell teachers exactly what instructional framework to use and the best strategies for every situation.	The coach's role is to engage teachers in meaningful conversations and facilitate discourse that moves teachers toward shared understanding of best teaching practices.
The role of the coach is to make managerial things easy for teachers by guiding them step by step through problems and serving as an extra pair of hands in the classroom.	The role of a coach is to provide support for teachers and promote perseverance in solving problems together.

One of the best parts of being a coach is being fully engaged with other educators in conversations about exceptional teaching, leading, and learning. I often find, though, that some who are expected to take on a coaching role are hesitant and unsure about how to do this work the "right way." They worry about offending people or being bossy. They worry about not having an administrative title that gives them authority. Coaching and giving feedback can make coaches feel nervous, afraid of doing the work wrong or not doing it well enough, or even of fearful being "found out" that they aren't actually an expert in everything. If you feel any of these things, believe me, I hear you. I've been there. But I'm here to tell you that you've got this. If you can concretely define your beliefs (make the implicit explicit) about your role as a coach, you will feel more secure and sincere in your relationship with teachers. That sincerity is the first step to building an important connection.

In this book, you'll see how all the pathways of the coaching connectome work together as a system, and you'll also notice the nuance associated with each pathway. Even as we discover these pathways, it's important to affirm something from the beginning:

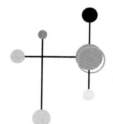

To be a good coach, you have to be sincere, authentic, and true to yourself—you quite simply have to be you!

You can learn a ton about how to coach from a myriad of experts out there, but at the end of the day, you need to take all of that learning and use it in your own unique way, like only you can do. So to be an exceptional coach, start by just being you.

Commit to developing a reflective sense of self and communication skills that empower and inspire others. Read articles, befriend mentors, learn from them. But coaching tools and strategies are just one of the aspects of the coaching connectome. Remember the central component of this phenomenal system is you—and the passion and purpose you bring.

SYNAPSE: SELF-REFLECTION

Write down your top three pieces of advice for incoming teachers, then look back and identify themes that emerge. What do those themes suggest about your experiences as an educator and what you've learned? What do they suggest about your expertise or your knowledge? This self-reflection helps you become a more sincere communicator.

1.

2.

3.

◆ THE IMPORTANCE OF PASSION

One thing I've learned from my own self-reflection is that I connect most with people over shared passions, because passion is part of how I stay motivated in my work. I always think of a story about Albert Einstein when he lived in Berlin and had just written his theory of general relativity. His eleven-year-old son was living with his mother in Vienna, and Einstein had decided to send him a letter. In it, he praises his son for pursuing the piano and advises him to "mainly play the things on the piano which please you," even if they are not what his teacher assigned. He goes on to observe:

That is the way to learn the most, that when you are doing something with such enjoyment that you don't notice that the time passes. I am sometimes so wrapped up in my work that I forget about the noon meal.

Do you ever get caught up in your coaching work so much that you forget to eat or you look at the clock and wonder where the day has gone? I do! I love the work of both teaching and learning and am deeply passionate about engaging with other adult learners in this work. I can get caught up in riveting planning sessions with teacher teams where we are working together to create special learning experiences for students. I am passionate about collaborative conversations with teachers where we come up with something new and creative to solve a problem or confront a challenge. I am also passionate about the belief in teachers and the power they have to help students accomplish amazing things. I am passionate about reading, listening to podcasts, and other resources that help us learn and grow in our craft. I am passionate about seeking out, highlighting, and nurturing the strengths we see in others even if they don't see them in themselves. I am passionate about building relationships with our colleagues that are grounded in trust and respect. I am passionate about designing authentic, relevant, and engaging professional learning opportunities for the adults with whom we work. I truly believe that being a part of a team of people coming around the table to brainstorm unique ways to grow in our craft in order to facilitate greater student learning is one of the best ways to spend our time.

Passion often gets the credit for why we get up in the morning. We tell ourselves, "I'm passionate about helping teachers, therefore I am motivated to work hard to go to work and be a great coach today." Some days you can easily tap into that passion, and when you do, it fills you with confidence, courage, and stamina to face whatever the day throws at you. We all love those days when we get to spend our time doing exactly what we love to do. But we also know there are days where we are frustrated, where we question why we're doing what we're doing, and when we try to tap into that passion, it's just not there. What happens then, when you feel discouraged and your passion seems to have disappeared?

◆ DISCOVER YOUR PURPOSE

One thing I'd like for you to consider is that we know we can't always rely on passion alone. But when we connect our passion with a deeply held purpose, we find we can get through even the toughest of days and bring sincerity back to our relationships with others. In *Everyday Instructional Coaching*, I highlight a connection between passion and purpose. *Passionate* is an adjective that receives a good amount of hype, as it should. It affirms an inner happiness and indicates pleasant emotions. However, passion can often be circumstantial and based on what excites someone at a particular point in his or her life.

Parts of life and work may be dull, challenging, or require self-discipline for us to deal with them. For example, there are days where we just don't feel like jumping into a collaborative planning meeting. Some days, it seems like every possible fire that could be started has started, leaving no time to plan that innovative professional development for your teachers. Or this is the second time this week that you were asked to sub for a teacher because the district doesn't have enough substitute teachers. Some days, we feel inspired, energized, and passionate because we were able to feel like we made an impact on a teacher or classroom. But we all know that some days require us to do things we don't feel like doing. We must create that form. We must email that teacher. We must create a new professional development aligned to our current environment. These things require us to have a strong purpose so we can endure them to achieve something larger. Passion can inspire, but without its connection to a deeply valued and rooted purpose, it won't create action.

I think a better way to think of this is *purpose-filled passion*. Using an approach of purpose-filled passion, we can reframe that frustrating experience of being asked to cover for a class again as an opportunity to practice a new instructional strategy. Reading to students becomes an opportunity to inspire.

Earlier in the chapter, we discussed aspects of coaching that fire us up and get us excited, but it's our purpose that gets us out of bed in the mornings. It's our purpose that carries us through the times when we feel weary, frustrated, or stuck. Our purpose is concise, yet powerful: to support teachers and to strengthen teacher practice by partnering with them. When you are able to articulate your passions and be sure of your purpose, you bring a renewed sincerity into your work with teachers.

SYNAPSE: DISCOVER YOUR PURPOSE

What is your purpose? To determine your purpose, answer these questions:

1. Why did you choose to be a coach?
2. What is it that you uniquely bring to the coaching profession?
3. Why must YOU coach?
4. What challenges are you willing to face because you have chosen to coach?
5. How is coaching bigger than yourself?

BEING VISIBLE TO EACH OTHER

What does it mean to be visible as a coach, to be fully immersed in the teacher-coach relationship? What makes coaches effective in immersing themselves in the school culture and communicating confidently? How can this immersion improve sincerity between coaches and teachers? A fully immersive and visible coach proudly accepts their own idiosyncrasies and quirks while recognizing that these things coexist with skills and experiences. Instructional coaches should examine their thoughts, opinions, and feelings without regard to popularity or acceptance. They should speak clearly and confidently because they have worked to develop a rich sense of self. Feeling and being fully visible means they love themselves well enough to believe that they are worthy of kindness and compassion from others without exception. When turbulent waves of conflict start to rock the boat when interacting with others, the reaction is simple and uncomplicated: display patience and sincerity while asserting positive intention. Be authentic, and be you. Free yourself from the idea that you have to be the expert in everything, recognize your strengths, and see strengths in others as well. Coaching is a partnership. Let go of your ego and your fear of "getting it wrong" or having to be perfect

Think about a time (hopefully the time is now) when you were working in a school and you were able to be completely yourself: The relationships you're building are genuine and sincere. After school, you walk down the hallway to a teacher friend's classroom to share a funny story that happened in your classroom today. And then you hear a story about a lightbulb moment in your colleague's classroom.

I remember one day when I was conducting a walkthrough as a school administrator. I was listening to a teacher explain the science concepts of motion and free fall. I had been a physics teacher and worked at NASA, so this concept was particularly interesting to me. I could tell that the teacher and probably the whole teacher team could benefit from a mini lesson on free fall, gravity, and force. So after school, I jumped into their teacher team meeting and essentially facilitated a small-group session. At one point I started drawing a triangle and using some trigonometry—and I got some puzzled looks from the teachers, as if I'd completely lost it. We all had a great laugh, and to this day, I'll still get messages about my "infamous triangles."

It's these stories that we remember. It's those conversations in the faculty lounge or before school during student drop-off duty. It's what your teacher friend across the hall made for dinner last night. It's the new flexible seating arrangement in your classroom you're proud of and showing off to everyone who comes by your room. It's hearing about a tough night one of your students had with a home situation. It's comforting a grieving student because she lost her grandfather.

These are the memories that stick with us after we've left the school building, moved on to a new position, or retired. These are the stories that connect us.

In her TED Talk, Jacqueline Novogratz talks about living a life of immersion. She shares stories of people she has met along the way and provides practical components of the greatest human aspiration: living a life of purpose. In her talk, she tells a story about a friend of hers who was part of a Native American tribe. The elders of this tribe, before they made decisions, would visualize the faces of their tribes seven generations in the future. Can you imagine what it would be like if we visualized seven generations in the future when we made decisions for our students? If we thought about how those students would be affected by the decisions made today? When we visualize the future, we're able to better identify circumstances or problems in our current reality and start to articulate the change we envision to someone else.

I found this quote to be one of the most compelling from Novogratz's talk: "What we really yearn for as human beings is to be visible to each other." There is so much truth to this. So why is it that we sometimes struggle to be visible to each other? Is it because we fear not being approachable or likable, we fear being embarrassed, or we fear being inferior? Later in this book I will address the differences between a collegial and productive coach-teacher relationship and being a friend. Coaches must earn respect and collegiality over time. Earning respect helps us all to overcome this fear, because we realize that being liked is not what we value. It's really respect.

There are still two other fears we often have to navigate: the fear of being embarrassed and the fear of feeling inferior. Because of the perceived role of the instructional coach as a master teacher, many of us place an unnecessary burden on ourselves to appear to have all the answers and know all the teaching strategies ever created. As coaches we work alongside teachers to illuminate strengths and partner with them to identify growth opportunities. But in the back of our minds, we may be wrestling with insecurities: "I've never taught that grade or subject," "I've never been a literacy specialist," or "I've never taught math." But teachers have these same insecurities about themselves: "Will the coach validate my opinions since I'm only a second-year teacher?" "Will the coach label me as old school and set in my ways because of my many years of experience?" "Will the coach think I'm an effective teacher after observing me?" Remember Novogratz's quote: "What we really yearn for as human beings is to be visible to each other." This is true only when we feel completely safe in the presence of someone else. We spend a lot of time in relationships putting up barriers or slowly dismantling them. Someone you trust immensely will have much easier access to your vulnerabilities than someone you don't. Think back on a time when a colleague broke your trust. You felt like you lowered your wall and this person took a chunk of it and hurled it back at you. So you built the wall back up to protect your emotional health and personal well-being. We can begin being more visible to our colleagues by giving them a window into our experiences. Tell a story about a time when you felt disappointed as a teacher. Tell a funny story about your first year as a teacher. Stories connect us. This not only conquers the fears of embarrassment and inferiority but also disarms the teacher so they can feel more comfortable in sharing insecurities.

 SYNAPSE

Pair up or get in a small group with your teachers and ask each other to share embarrassing moments or moments of professional failure. Then reflect on how those moments provided opportunities for growth. Also make connections for teachers about how this activity builds sincerity.

◆ *PROFESSIONAL LEARNING*

Another aspect of immersion is the capacity to boost a culture of life-long learning. As a coach, I want each person to know I value them and the work they do, and I also want to be seen as someone who adds value to their work. I want them to know that I'm a learner, that I support their learning and growth, and that I can be a valuable resource in helping them on their own personal learning journey. One of the things I always did as an administrator when I was reading something new is keep note of who I thought might like the article, book, or whatever I was reading. I started early on with a simple sticky-note system and ultimately evolved to using Evernote and "tagging" the articles, blog posts etc. When the opportunity would arise, I'd make sure to get a copy of the reading to the person I thought might enjoy it, and I'd make a point of sharing with them why I thought they in particular might enjoy it or how it might enhance their work. There were things I found that I thought we should read together as an entire staff, but also things I found that were unique to specific people based on what I knew they were working on at the time. Knowing what each person might like or find valuable typically came from being in their classrooms and noticing when they were trying something new or from being engaged in collaborative conversations about their practice.

While this practice started as a simple way for me to share my own learning path, there was an added benefit to it. It strengthened the relationships and rapport with my team because the sharing and support was often personalized. A conversation might start like this:

> You just shared with me last week that you were wanting to build in more time for small-group instruction and were interested in designing more meaningful tasks for the students who were working independently during your small-group time. I just came across this article on literacy stations that has some amazing examples of independent and small-group activities that students can do on their own or in pairs or triads. Some of them seem really engaging and have great potential to help sharpen literacy skills. I thought of you immediately and thought you might like to read it. When you do, I'd love to hear what you think!

Statements like the one above, when heartfelt and genuine, say to someone "I see you," "I'm thinking about you," "I support you," and "I'm making time for you." All of these feelings contribute to strong, positive relationships. When I moved to the district office, I used the same practice with the principals and coaches I supported, often sharing articles and resources with them that I knew they might find valuable based on visits and the many collaborative conversations we would have as well.

 SYNAPSE

1. Choose at least two people on your team and share a personalized resource with them. (It would be awesome if you choose them because you noticed something they were working on or they shared something with you in your collaborative conversation.)

2. Tell them specifically why you thought of them.

3. Enthusiastically end the conversation with, "After you read this, I'd love to hear your thoughts!" This opens the door for another collaborative conversation and possibly a chance to offer support.

4. A few thoughts:

   • Don't just drop an article in their box without saying anything about it—it doesn't have the same personal touch.

   • Don't use this practice as a substitute for having a courageous conversation about ineffective practices.

   • Don't attach a deadline to reading the article or perusing the resource. No one wants to feel like you are assigning them homework.

CULTURE OF RAPPORT

I learned my biggest lesson on rapport from being a school administrator. As a school leader, a big part of my day was calling parents. I called parents to brag about students learning, their academic achievement, or some wonderful choice they made in the hallway or lunchroom. I also had to call parents about misbehavior that warranted administrator involvement.

One of the biggest lessons I learned as a school leader was that it was more important to support students with self-regulation skills than adhere to a traditional discipline framework. There are other social-emotional-behavior practices that provide long-term improvement by focusing on positives, reinforcing and redirecting teacher language, and logical consequences to help students develop positive behaviors.

There were some days where I had so many parent phone calls to make it that it felt rote and robotic. "Hi Mr. or Mrs. Smith, how are you? I'm calling to share with you that Susie had a tough day in class today." I would proceed to share what happened and how the behavior was managed. When you have thirty calls to make in an afternoon, it starts to feel like a to-do list, and not like you're addressing the root problem.

There needed to be a different approach to supporting teachers with practices that invest students in classroom expectations, involve student goal setting, and incorporate structured reflection and self-regulation. As I began to work with specific classrooms on these more empowering approaches, something else became evident. I needed to invest more into the school-parent relationship. Parents know the educators who are truly present, investing in their kids, and investing in them as parents.

A morning greeting every morning to parents and students was so important. Being visible in the lunchroom and talking with parents eating with their kids was a game changer. These interactions will always be more important than that meeting you have to get to or that phone call you have to return. These interactions bring me back to my core as an educator and my purpose. Creating a pathway to sincerity requires you to build rapport with all stakeholders as it relates to your purpose.

To get to a place where teachers feel completely comfortable sharing concerns and fears, we must establish a working definition of rapport. Teachers know the leaders that are truly present and are investing in them. They notice the leaders and coaches that are just checking boxes on their to-do list by walking through their class really quickly or holding the obligatory faculty meeting. Rapport can't be faked. It can't be rushed. You can't just declare you have a rapport with your teachers. Rapport must be created, developed, and nurtured over time. Rapport starts with investing in people. What does this look like?

- **Attitude.** The attitude with which you do things is more important than checking off the thing. Teachers can tell the difference when you're sincere about the support you're providing them and when you're just checking a box. What is your posture like? Are you smiling? What is your language like? Does it say "I'm happy to do this" or "I have to do this"?
- **Presence.** When you're meeting with teachers, are you actively engaged? Are you a true partner? Are you asking questions? Are you actively listening? Are you communicating back to the teacher the message you perceived? Are you truly collaborative or simply waiting to say what you think?
- **Feedback.** The quality of the feedback and the process you've established is indicative of the kind of rapport you have with your teachers. Are your questions tied more to student success than a teacher's personality? Are you analyzing data and patterns together? Are you helping the teacher synthesize learning, draw conclusions and set next steps? Are you helping the teacher with conclusions that we can draw regarding the success of their students?
- **Appreciation.** When you start a conversation with a teacher, what do you say first? Are you starting from a place of appreciation? There are so many things we can observe in a classroom that we can and should appreciate about a teacher's practice and decision-making. Look for it. Communicate it. Start conversations from a place of appreciation and strength as opposed to with what you perceived as needing to be fixed.

- **Lack of Assumptions and Judgment.** When you observe a classroom, you only see the minutes you see. You don't see what came before you walked in, and you don't see what happens after you go. So don't make assumptions. If you have questions, ask them! And leave your judgment at the door. Teaching is an incredibly complex craft. It is never about what you as the coach liked or didn't like or what YOU would do differently. It is about supporting teachers' lessons in a way that honors who they are while infusing sound pedagogical practices to positively impact student learning.

Helping to make school a place of mutual respect, not just for students but for staff as well, is incredibly important to us in our roles as coaches. Building rapport brings out the best in our teams and creates a culture where people not only want to work, but they want to do their BEST work.

Below are ten ways you can help create rapport in your school:

- See the value and the contributions that each person brings to your team and point it out to them often.
- Establish clear goals, set high expectations, and give everyone time and support to achieve them.
- Equip your team with the learning and resources they need to be successful.
- Treat people as both experts and expert learners.
- Expect people to work with you rather than for you.
- Afford people autonomy and trust.
- Embrace mistakes as a necessary part of working with other humans.
- Discover what each person is passionate about and what matters to them. Tap into those passions whenever you can.
- Give people the gift of your time and undivided attention.
- Respect people as well-rounded individuals who have important priorities beyond their work.

 ## SYNAPSE

Of the ten ways provided to help create rapport with your staff:

1. Choose the top three ways from the list that would have the biggest impact on your school staff. These will be the first three you'll focus on before moving to the others.

2. Turn these into actionable goals. For example:

   "I will afford people with autonomy and trust by implementing a pineapple-chart observation protocol in the teacher's lounge. Teachers get to sign up to observe other teachers doing cool things. There is no expectation, debrief, or form, it's purely a no-stakes and fun way to observe other teachers doing awesome things."

3. Make a plan to be intentional about focusing on the three goals and create a timeline for implementation. For example:

   "Pineapple chart communicated, established, and posted by next Monday."

4. Be purposeful throughout the week to ensure you're working on building rapport.

5. At the end of the week, reflect on progress you made toward the goals. For example:

   "I recorded a quick video about the pineapple chart and sent it to my fellow colleagues. I've received a lot of positive feedback thus far. I will print a chart and encourage teachers to sign up tomorrow."

You can use the following template to work on your rapport goals:

Rapport goals for the week of _____
1.   2.   3 .
Action steps based on goals: 1.   2.   3 .
Reflection/progress on goals:

The goal is to get to a place where each person on the team has other team members who care enough about them to be honest rather than telling them what they want to hear. We do not want people to just blindly agree with each other no matter what. In a team with high rapport, every team member values you—not despite your imperfections but because of them. When a pathway of sincerity has been constructed, we are all okay with pointing things out (and okay with things being pointed out to us) when we have messed up because we will also support others (and want to be supported) to fix it or solve it.

PATHWAY OF CONFIDENCE

FRAMING THE COACHING RELATIONSHIP

What if we don't mesh? What if my ideas aren't received well? What if I come off too strong? What if I'm shy? These are the kinds of questions we all ask ourselves when initializing a new relationship. Thinking about cultivating relationships can be a bit nerve-racking and overwhelming. In this section, we'll explore how you tap into and build on your confidence as a coach and how confidence applies to the coach-teacher relationship.

It's not surprising to hear that coaching is all about relationships; the concept is baked into the job description. But at some juncture between the beginning of the school year and that first preconference meeting of the coaching cycle, we've already begun to focus on checking off the to-dos on our list. We are thrust into this cycle just two weeks into the beginning of school. What happened to the organic and sincere relationship that was supposed to be cultivated over time?

First of all, let's establish what this relationship is to begin with. When we hear the word *relationship*, we often go straight to the idea of *friendship*. We think about what a relationship could look like: a person being our ally, a loyal supporter, a cheerleader, and always on our side. The meaning, structure, form, and function of a relationship often seems fluid and ambiguous. Even the very process of defining it makes it feel insincere and inorganic. In our current culture, we hear the word *friend* used for peers we just met on Twitter or a new acquaintance at work. Mutual adoration or shared interest often gets dubbed *friendship*.

Friends are those people we are bound to because of shared personal experiences and those with whom we have the deepest level of emotional and cognitive intimacy. They are the people we might have a Zoom meeting with before we get our hair fixed, the people we share embarrassing moments with, and the people with whom we can share our unpopular thoughts with without any fear of judgment or fear of a loss of affection.

If we're honest, most connections in our school building are not friendships; they are professional acquaintances with respected colleagues. That might seem a little bit stuffy and formal. Acquaintances would be those you say are in your PLN (professional learning network). These are people you like, speak to, and might see every day. You know how long they've taught and some of their hobbies. You might even know their favorite color is blue or that they went to Cabo for summer vacation. You have positive interactions with them during team meetings or at lunchtime.

As a coach, your mission is not to make everyone your friend. (In fact, given the framing of friendship we've described above, that would be impossible.) Over time, some of those relationships might evolve into friendships, while others will stay acquaintanceships. That is okay. Your mission is to be a trusted partner in education. A co-collaborator and thought partner. Someone who will question and solve problems alongside teachers. Someone who will actively listen and will empathize. A coach's goal is to have a collaborative and productive relationship with teachers.

I remember the first instructional coach I had as a first-year teacher. I was young, naive, energetic, and a bit threatened that a veteran educator of thirty years was going to be in my classroom. Would she tell me what I was doing wrong? Would she appreciate my teaching style? Would she judge my classroom management?

All of my fears were quickly alleviated upon the first time I met her. I vividly recall her coming into my classroom right after school one day. She was kind, polite, and casual. She affirmed my teaching style and told me she had heard that students really enjoyed being in my classroom. That felt great to hear. Then she got right to it. She defined her role and asked what she could do to best support me. She described for me the kind of work we would be doing together and asked for my input. Her demeanor and the collaborative process she described immediately reduced the anxiety I had about the teacher-coach experience. This set in motion the beginning of a collaborative and effective coach-teacher relationship. Her confidence in herself as a coach helped strengthen my own confidence as a teacher.

◆ COMMUNICATION IS KEY

You can set the tone for a confident, effective, and productive coach-teacher relationship with good communication. To do that, as a coach, you must be intentional about having a framing conversation early to discuss the structure and processes that will support the coach-teacher relationship.

Below is an example of a framing conversation:

Coach: Hi. It is great to meet you, thank you for taking time to chat today. Before we get started, I want to let you know about some of the things I hope we will accomplish in our meeting today. I hope we can learn a bit about each other, talk about the structure of our work together, and talk through any questions you might have. I am also looking forward to learning more about you and your work in education. I want to share a little about me and my role. It is important that we also talk about what you hope to get out of this partnership so that we can make sure it is productive and relevant for you moving forward.

(Coach and teacher take ten minutes to share little about each other and their experiences in education.)

Coach: I'd like to learn a little bit more about you as a science teacher before we embark on this journey together. Why did you decide to become a teacher?

(Teacher shares. Coach actively listens, asks clarifying questions.)

Coach: As a coach, I am your thought partner and collaborator. I'll help you look at your practice with an extra set of lenses and through a position of support. I can also help you identify areas for growth. My role is not to tell you what you should do but to help guide you through the process of looking at teacher practice and student learning, and to discuss specific strategies. You have a very exciting background, and I know that I will always learn something new from you along the way. What do you hope to gain and how do you see yourself in this relationship?

(This will take five minutes.)

Coach: I'm really looking forward to working together this year. You might be familiar with the instructional coaching framework (provide a copy) and the coaching cycle. We will have goal-setting meetings, scheduled observations, modeling sessions, and debriefs. In my experience, one of the most important factors in ensuring a productive and positive experience is sticking to a consistent schedule. The next time we meet, we'll find a time on our calendars to have a regular sync up. This will be thirty minutes every other week that is set aside for our conversations on a schedule we can be confident about sticking to without giving it away to anyone or anything else. Can you think of a time like that when you have access to a quiet and private space, away from interruptions and distractions?

(Discuss potential days and times for schedule.)

Coach: What questions do you have about me or our plan going forward?

(Answer any questions and thank them again for their time.)

You'll notice that this example framing conversation is not lengthy. You don't want the first conversation to be overwhelming. You want to keep it concise, professional, and positive. The coach's underlying demeanor and dispositions should be characterized by kindness, empathy, mutual respect, and a focus on achievement of professional goals. This approach minimizes any potential negative personal factors that may get in the way of a collegial and collaborative relationship. And it will also boost the teacher's confidence in you.

SYNAPSE

When you are beginning the school year or have a new teacher on staff, kick off new relationships with a framing conversation with the following elements:

- Warm greeting
- Clearly laid-out expectations
- Coach and teacher both share a little about their experiences in education
- Coach clarifies the role and asks the teacher, "What do you hope to gain and how do you see yourself in this relationship?"
- Coach to provide brief overview of instructional coaching framework (or coaching cycle process)
- Discuss potential days and times for schedule

- Coach will answer any questions and thank teacher for their time

Don't forget to document the teacher's name, day, time, and any notes from the framing conversation.

RELATIONSHIP AS A PROCESS

The world of education has become very good at measuring achievement, outcomes, deliverables, etc. Because coaching is inherently tied to student learning, we already must fight against coaching becoming a matter of compliance and obligation. Relationship-building is a process and requires time and experience to provide a natural closeness between humans. The coaching relationship also relies on a process so that coaching can be productive.

We need the coaching relationship to be productive so that it has a direct impact on student learning. But productivity can produce a higher yield when presence becomes the focus of coaching. If the coach-teacher relationship has only the aim of launching the coaching cycle—without allowing trust and warmth to develop—it won't lead to the most productive outcome. Yes, the coach can check off "preconference" and "observation" from their list (sounds productive), but we know that checking things off a list doesn't yield real results.

A rewarding and productive coach-teacher relationship is not something that happens overnight, and that should not be the goal. It reminds me of planting bulbs. I live in Maine, so once I get to late April and early May, I am ready to see the flowers erupt. After six months of cold and snow, the first signs of tulips, daffodils, crocuses, and hyacinths are such a wonderful sight. But if I want flowers to emerge, I must plant the bulbs and tubers of these plants in the fall. The success of these flowers is in the planting and the waiting. They must be placed at a certain depth, with some bulb food and some water. They must also be planted in the middle of autumn, when the ground is cool but before it freezes. The cold temperatures are necessary for dormancy, so that these bulbs can grow into beautiful flowers in the spring. Success in May is due to the care provided when planting in October. Similarly, the coach-teacher relationship takes time and requires the challenge of working together before the confidence that comes from success later on can blossom.

A note about the coach-teacher relationship: nobody wants to be fixed. That implies that we're broken, that we aren't good enough, that others are better than us. We know we don't want to be fixed ourselves, and we know very few other people who want to be. We do, though, love to learn and grow, and most other adults do, too. A teacher won't really be confident in a coach who treats them like they need to be fixed. Helping teachers learn and grow, however, will also boost confidence in the coach. Those of us who serve in leadership and coaching roles, though, might unintentionally convey to people that we are trying to fix them as opposed to partnering with them on a learning journey. In our urgency to make things better, we often have a tendency to look around our campuses and inside our classrooms seeing all of the problems we want to tackle, the things that need tending to, the things that need fixing. While this mentality works great when it comes to a broken laptop or an unsafe swing on the playground, it does not work with people! Teachers are smart, accomplished professionals. They see right through us when we come into their classrooms with our "fix it" mentality.

Now that the coach and teacher have co-established and defined the tone and vision for the relationship (trusting, organic, nonjudgmental, present, and collegial), these processes and structures will be the framework upon which confident coaching will occur. This framework must be directly tied to students' needs. In education we say this phrase a lot. What's an example of a coaching framework that's a byproduct of students' needs? We know that students must have a sense of belonging, safety, and security before deep learning can occur. We also know that students must be able to connect their intrinsic motivations to learning objectives if they are to engage with learning at the highest levels. Therefore, a coaching framework would be constructed to ensure teachers are also collaborating in an environment that is conducive to their learning (one with safety, security, and belonging). All unit planning would ensure that students are making intrinsic connections and not just doing work out of compliance. It's important that we know our students' and teachers' needs before we construct an instructional coaching framework.

FINDING CONFIDENCE AND FIGHTING SELF-DOUBT

At some point, all of us will feel insecure or have self-doubt creep up on us. It's not a matter of if but when—and how we respond to it. I have found there are times in life when it's easy to arm yourself with the confidence you need to move forward. And at other times, that confidence goes missing. As a part of my career, I've written books and given hundreds of—if not a thousand—presentations. You would think that from those experiences I'd have received plenty of affirmation to give me confidence. But I've found there is no correlation between the number of accolades you receive and the level of insecurity you experience at any point in time. Confidence, instead, is a choice. It's not innate. It's not based on prior performance. It's a deliberate choice to be you, wonderfully and uniquely you.

We have all been there: a situation where someone criticizes you for not having a certain experience or credential and therefore attempts to invalidate your opinion, solution, and thinking around a situation. I had it happen as a young principal, as I had to evaluate teachers who had been teaching much longer than I had. It has probably happened to you. Maybe you were a middle school English teacher before you became a coach, and now you're coaching an elementary teacher and providing feedback about a math lesson. Or you've been in education for thirty years and you're giving advice to a first-year teacher who had a completely different teacher-training experience. How could we possibly engender trust and credibility in a teacher when they realize we have not been in their shoes?

There is a piece of research that can help us tackle this very consequential and real issue. It was carried out by Polman and Emich (2011). In a study, people were asked to imagine a prisoner locked away in a high tower. All they have available to help them escape is a rope that is only half as long as the drop from the tower's window. Even so, they still manage to escape from the tower by dividing the rope in half and tying it back together. How is that possible? Participants in this study were given two different versions of this puzzle. Half of them were given this version, while the other half were told to imagine it was they who were imprisoned in the tower. Both groups then had to explain how the escape was made. In the group that were told it was a nameless "prisoner" who was stuck in the tower, 66 percent of people got the answer right. However, when told to imagine they were stuck in the tower themselves, only 48 percent of participants got the right solution. The reason for this discrepancy can be explained by how the mind visualizes problems like this. When we think about someone else in the high tower, our minds tend to think more abstractly. In this abstract mode, creative thinking is easier because we aren't preoccupied by our own welfare. (Oh, in case you're wondering, the solution to the prisoner scenario is this: the rope is divided in half width-ways rather than length-ways. Then you can halve the width and double the length.)

We can use this fact as coaches when we encounter the statement, "Well you can't advise or coach me because you haven't done this or that..." Yes, we *can* actually. We can partner alongside a teacher because we are less encumbered by the situation or circumstance they're in. Remember: you establish your credibility by being yourself, period. Not some degree, piece of paper, experience, or title.

◆ JOURNALING

One of the best ways you can successfully navigate self-doubt is through journaling. Maybe you've tried journaling before and didn't find it helpful. Or maybe you journaled before and now feel like you don't have time like you used to. But no matter how busy you are, you can prioritize journaling. The easiest way to journal consistently is make a habit out of it. Can you make it a part of your morning routine while you sip your coffee? Or at night as you're getting into bed? I have found that journaling can be one of the best fifteen minutes of my day. (If you're looking for a good journal, I'd recommend *Journal like a PIRATE*).

How does journaling help with self-doubt? First of all, if you decide to journal daily then you've already created a tool for self-discipline. Journals can become a sounding board for much-needed affirmations and positive self-talk in the face of constant doubt. You know yourself better than anyone, so this is your opportunity to tell yourself how amazing you are.

SYNAPSE: JOURNALING

To get started, you can always begin with "I am," "I have," or "I can" prompts:

- I am grateful for my home.
- I am thankful for my spouse, partner, significant other, friends, and/or family.
- I am a great coach and teacher.
- I am a caring educator.
- I can speak to my colleagues with confidence and courage.
- I can choose how I spend my day.
- I am in excellent health.
- I have access to an abundance of food choices.

Use this same approach to write about each of the following areas:

- Physical health and well-being
- Family and friends
- Education
- Relationships at work
- Leisure and self-care activities
- Finances

Additionally, a diary can keep you accountable and moving forward despite the number of disruptions, to-dos, meetings, and responsibilities you have. You can and will always find an excuse not to write. We do the same with exercise, cleaning the house, and countless other things we should do. But here is the reality: the very act of acknowledging all of the externals vying for your attention or the forces trying to derail your work and goals but still deciding to journal anyway emboldens you and boosts your confidence, conquering that self-doubt. You look at the journal, and even if it's the only thing you've been disciplined about today, it feels like a win.

Resist the urge to measure yourself in your journal. Only you are reading it. Be 100 percent honest and raw with yourself. A journal isn't some collection of perfect entries highlighting how you're the best and the greatest educator or human in the word. It's a beautiful journey into your soul, bearing your mistakes, failures, flaws, and missteps. And that is the most human endeavor ever. Being willing to be honest with yourself is in and of itself an act of courage.

As I close this chapter about confidence, I want to leave you with this. What makes you an exceptional human and educator is that even though you are constantly bombarded with feelings of self-doubt, you still choose to move forward anyway. This feeling-action cycle is what sets you apart. You don't allow self-doubt to rule you or keep you from taking that risk. You still show up and do the work. Because at the end of the day, when you place your head on your pillow, you feel the pride and peace knowing you did your very best today. That's the success. It's in the work itself.

PATHWAY OF CULTURE

THE POWER OF LANGUAGE

When someone says the words "Nilla Wafer" or "saltine cracker," visual and taste memories come to my mind. Growing up in the South, I ate banana pudding topped with Nilla Wafers. Hearing that word makes me think of family reunions, potlucks, and summer. When I think of a saltine cracker, I have unpleasant thoughts. I'm reminded of being sick to my stomach and eating crackers to settle it. Others may have fonder memories, like eating crackers with chili or with a warm bowl of soup on a cold winter day. The same thing happens in school: our everyday language triggers very specific emotions, thoughts, and actions. Language is very powerful in creating positive change and in completely establishing a collegial culture. Using it that way takes purpose and displays intentionality. The words and tone we choose can build respect, influence, and trust with teachers, helping us disarm any aversion to change. Additionally, our language is meant to empower teacher voice in the decision-making process. Being intentional with our language is pivotal in our growth as a coach. We may be able to create a pathway connection that gives a teacher hope if we are comfortable enough to use the right language and say things like "Are you struggling?" It's possible that by using the right language, we can create a new culture pathway in our connection.

It's important to have exemplars around what a positive conversation looks and sounds like within the many contexts of the school day.

Context	Looks like...	Sounds like...
Coaching Cycle	Teachers are actively working, exploring their chosen goals.	Teachers are inquiring, discussing, and conjecturing.
Team Meetings	Teachers are interacting in a collaborative way. There is a palpable energy and excitement.	Teachers are presenting ideas, affirming each other, and providing feedback.
Debriefing	Active nonverbals: smiling, thinking, scratching head, nodding, responding.	Respectful conversations with affirming tones and self-responsibility.
Facilitating Professional Development	Active nonverbals: smiling, nodding, responding, etc.	Teachers are asking questions focused on the learning outcomes and their intrinsic interests.

Communicating with purposeful language also means that we recognize and affirm teachers in meaningful ways, frequently, and consistently for taking actions that have real value. Every time you walk through a classroom, teachers want your affirmation and feedback. Think about times when you have been affirmed by persons whom you respect. How did those words of affirmation affect your own sense of dedication and motivation? But the way people think about their intelligence has a marked influence on their motivation to learn. A growth mindset exists when one believes he or she can learn and grow every day and that their beliefs aren't static. Those with a fixed mindset think that the way they see the world remains locked in place. Dweck (2006) concludes that when educators praise students for their intellectual ability, it doesn't increase motivation and resilience but instead encourages a fixed mindset. In contrast, praising students for the effort they put forth and how they process learning (through reasoning, communication, perseverance, strategy, improvement, etc.) promotes sustainable motivation. It tells students what they've done to succeed and what they need to do to succeed again in the future.

We can apply Dweck's growth-mindset research to adult learners—all educators—who have a desire to continually learn, grow, and experience personal and professional success. Coaches should learn new skills and engage in new experiences alongside teachers. Coaches should highlight their own failures as they happen and focus on how they learned from those experiences in the process of seeking a growth mindset. Coaches should also foster a culture of affirmation that is based on effort and not intelligence to promote that growth mindset in teachers.

GIVING EFFECTIVE FEEDBACK

In cultures that positively thrive in communication and transparency, giving effective feedback is one of the clear front runners. Coaches typically engage in walkthroughs as part of an agreed-on partnership or coaching cycle or as part of a daily process that's been previously communicated to teachers. Walkthroughs typically involve a brief appearance in the classroom for the purpose of taking the pulse of instructional effectiveness or to capture evidence of learning (or the lack thereof).

As coaches, we're really so careful not to judge or be evaluative in our feedback, and therefore sometimes we send ambiguous messages to the teacher. Too often, no subsequent feedback or affirmation occurs after short walkthroughs in the classroom, or coaches offer only minimal feedback. A coach may base the minimal feedback on something positive he or she witnessed, such as, "Your students could articulate the learning objective." However, if a coach gave more constructive feedback, it might sound like: "I wasn't sure of the lesson objective, nor did I see it posted." Constructive, transparent feedback should be an inherent part of the observation process.

To ensure feedback is effective and productive, teachers and coaches must have an agreed-on process for feedback and a clear strategy for how to give it. When a coach and a teacher co-develop student-success outcomes and classroom "look-fors" (predetermined pieces of evidence that align to instructional goals), they form a mutual agreement on the kinds of evidence that the coach will collect. A shared document provides a great way to communicate and track walkthrough data. The coach creates this living document with the teacher, and each time the coach engages with the classroom, he or she addresses a simple checklist, a narrative, or another agreed-on indicator. The teacher doesn't have to wait for a feedback email to come late at night or the next day; the coach's feedback updates immediately in the document.

The table below is a Coaching Conversation Debrief Guide. This guide is helpful after you've observed a full lesson.

COACHING CONVERSATION DEBRIEF GUIDE
A suggested sequence for a postlesson debrief conversation
1. Overall impression: • What was the tone of the student interactions throughout the lesson? • How successful were your students? • How successful was your attempt at implementing [name of strategy]? • Describe the strategies you used to support students.

2. Teacher data:
   - What was the goal of the lesson?
   - In what ways did your students meet or not meet your learning goals?
   - How do you know?
   - What is your evidence?

3. Collaboratively analyze data from coach:
   - Let's look at the observation data I collected.
   - What do you see?
   - What questions do you have about the data I collected?
   - What patterns can we find?
   - What does this tell us?

4. Conclusions and next steps:
   - What conclusions can we draw regarding the success of your students?
   - What conclusions can we draw regarding your implementation of [name of strategy]?
   - What are your long- and short-term goals?
   - What might your next steps be for supporting your students?
   - What additional resources might help you meet the needs of your students?

5. Reflect on the process:
   - How has this conversation helped you focus on your students?
   - What feedback do you have for me about this process?

◆ HOW TO GIVE BALANCED FEEDBACK

Feedback is a touchy subject, even beyond the school building. Even when we have agreed-upon processes and classroom look-fors, feedback can often feel subjective to the person who is receiving it, especially a relationship hasn't been previously established. And it's often still a tender subject, even when there is a relationship. You want the person to whom you're giving feedback to feel like you have their back and you're on their side. The last thing you want is for the other person to feel attacked.

Teachers will be much more open to criticism when they believe it's intended to help them and that you're on their side. Many of us have been given the advice that to give feedback, we should serve up a "feedback sandwich" as it is referred to by many feedback gurus. It starts with a slice of praise on the top and the bottom and places the filling of criticism in between. The only issue with this is that the person receiving the feedback senses what's happening, so they might just tune you out and only tune in when you get to the negative critique. That's because people are more likely to focus on and remember negative feedback than positive. Just think back on the times when you received feedback. You could be given ninety-nine pieces of positive feedback, but the negative feedback is the one that has the biggest impact on you and is the one you'll carry with you. Here is an example of how a feedback sandwich plays out in a coach-teacher conversation.

Situation: Sharice (teacher) and Jayda (coach) are having their postobservation debrief.

Jayda: Hi Sharice, thank you for inviting me into your classroom. Overall, I've been very impressed with student engagement in your classroom this school year. That being said, I think there are some opportunities for growth. I think you can work on your questioning strategies. When I've been in your classroom, I've noticed that most of the questions come from you instead of students. I've also noticed that you tend to call on the students who raise their hands, instead of calling on nonvolunteers. Let's work on that. I've noticed that your questions tend to be posed in the whole-group setting but not necessarily in small groups, where students seem to work independently. These are some things I'd like you to consider. Again, Sharice, really great work on making the classroom fun and engaging!

Let's analyze the feedback given above. Notice that the first and last sentences are the only areas of positive feedback, but that the feedback is basically the same thing said twice. Additionally, the positive feedback isn't very specific or helpful. What is it about the teacher's classroom environment or the relationship with her students that makes the classroom engaging and fun? Did you notice that the negative feedback, however, was very detailed and cited specific examples of when questioning wasn't effective? What would Sharice leave the meeting thinking about? She would be thinking about the negative feedback around her questioning and not about the positive comments about student engagement.

Instead of using the feedback sandwich, I recommend the Balanced Feedback strategy, developed by Randall Stutman (2020), instead. Balanced Feedback requires a person to give both positive and negative feedback in equally vivid, elaborate, and detailed manners.

Here's how Jayda would utilize the Balanced Feedback Framework to change the feedback to Sharice.

Jayda: Hi Sharice, thank you for inviting me into your classroom. Overall, I've been very impressed with student engagement in your classroom this school year. Students are eager to engage in learning, many are smiling and happy to talk about what they're working on. When I went around the classroom, many students knew the learning objective and understood how the activity tied to the learning standard. Additionally, many students were proud of their creations and they immediately wanted to show what they had done to create their project. Thank you for the positive energy you display in your classroom, as it has a direct impact on student motivation and helps create a classroom environment conducive for learning. I would like for teachers to come and observe you, to see the positive and respectful classroom environment you've created.

Let's talk about some opportunities for growth. When I've been in your classroom, I've noticed that most of the questions come from you instead of students. Allowing students to ask questions builds even deeper inquiry and higher levels of cognition. I've also noticed that you tend to call on the students who raise their hands, instead of calling on nonvolunteers. Do you notice that? I've noticed that your questions tend to be posed in the whole-group setting but not necessarily in small groups, where students seem to work independently. How can I help support you with some questioning strategies?

If we dig into this feedback, we can see that the positive and negative feedback are equal in terms of number as well as specificity and quality. This type of feedback requires a lot more intention and preparation from the coach. Instead of only noticing the areas of opportunity or growth, coaches have to equally notice the positive and standout areas.

Throughout this process, both teachers and coaches solve problems related to a collective commitment or goal while providing feedback to each other along the way. Because many conversations about a particular lesson or instructional practice can happen over a period of time, it helps to track the interactions with a regularly updated feedback-reflection tool, which can be as simple as a document shared in Google Docs. Teachers and coaches should use these tools to support their reflections on a weekly basis. This ensures the conversations are actionable and they do not get lost in the hustle and busyness of the day.

To promote accountability and transparency, all teachers should have the ability to see the coach's completed reflections (via a shared, collaborative document). The reflection tool's simple design and explicit prompts provide teachers with a quick and easy to see summative reflection that aids in decision-making.

How have I helped move ___ grade-level team toward a collective vision and to create norms that reflect the collective commitments to the work?
Notes:
I have supported the ___ team to be productive and to work cohesively to meet the common learning outcomes.
Notes:

I have supported the ___ team in designing quality common formative assessments that meet the rigor of the standards and employ common scoring agreements for each assessment.
Notes:
I have supported the ___ team in analyzing data from common formative assessments by standard and then supported teams in collective student reengagement in learning.
Notes:
I have supported the ___ team in identifying the instructional strategies that impact student learning for replication in future units or next year.
Notes:
I have supported the ___ team in helping them create a process of identifying students who do not meet, meet, or exceed essential learning standards and assisting the team in collectively creating a plan to ensure learning standards for all students.
Notes:

Notice the prompts in this reflection tool are focused around "support." As the coach, you aren't creating the formative assessments alone, nor are you identifying all the students who are not meeting learning standards. You, as the coach, are leading and supporting teams by helping them create effective processes and practices to do the important work. Additionally, the beauty of making this reflection form collaborative is that it provides an open invitation to two-way dialogue that doesn't only occur during a debrief. Feedback can occur both asynchronously through a collaborative digital document or synchronously through an impromptu conversation. An intentional and consistent feedback culture is framed around the premise that the coach and the teacher work together toward the same ultimate goal: to improve teacher practice and ultimately increase student learning. It's important for coaches to also ask for feedback. Coaches must continually ask for and seek feedback from teachers to establish this practice as a natural collaborative norm. We all see things through different lenses; therefore, the teacher and the coach have an invaluable opportunity to grow as feedback providers throughout the process.

SYNAPSE: MAKING TIME FOR OBSERVATIONS AND FEEDBACK

"How many observations should I be conducting per week?"

I get this question a lot from coaches. What if I said you should aim for forty observations per week? "Wait, what? That's impossible!" you say. It's actually not. It's part of a powerful and effective strategy for building a cycle of improvement and making feedback an embedded practice. That's because most of these observations are short, unannounced, and explicitly about learning and professional growth.

Now that it has sunk in a little, let's do the math.

Remember, forty—short—observations per week is our target. If you visit forty classrooms per week for five minutes each, you'll need two hundred minutes.

We know school hours vary a bit, but let's use an 8:00–3:00 school day for our purposes. That would be a seven-hour day, which equates to 420 minutes. So, two hundred minutes is not quite one-half of one school day. In fact, it is just forty minutes per day over five days.

And you really do have the time, because you prioritize it! You have forty minutes per day to do this impactful work, work that makes coaches and schools successful. You may even have sixty minutes! The next step is to block out the time on your calendar—two hundred minutes per week. This must be a priority and not scheduled over or canceled. I'm waiting. Go ahead and block it off now.

(The sound of you on your computer calendar creating observation blocks.)

Now that you have that time blocked off on your calendars, there is a bit more I need to tell you. You will also couple these spontaneous observations focused on learning and professional growth with direct and immediate feedback. So you do need some additional time to provide feedback.

I believe every observation deserves feedback. You don't need to have thirty-minute conversations about your five-minute observations. You can have highly effective conversations and give valuable feedback in three minutes or less. It takes practice, but I promise you can. Let's do some more math. Let's use three minutes for feedback for each of your forty-minute observations. That comes out to 120 minutes per week that you need to block off to give feedback to the people you observed.

Add that to your two hundred minutes and our grand total is 320 minutes. These 320 minutes per week can dramatically transform your school. If it's important, make time for it. This is important. Make time for it!

A healthy culture derives from a positive and purposeful plan for feedback between administrators, coaches, and teachers. Without feedback, schools remain stuck in ineffective practices for teaching and learning. Effective feedback structures help to shape culture by allowing educators the freedom to be vulnerable and to embrace mistakes as a natural part of learning and growing. They illuminate teacher's strengths, giving them the confidence to navigate uncharted paths.

COMPLIANCE CULTURE

Why are we still talking about compliance-leaning culture in schools today? Schools were based on an industrial-era model, but that era has been over for decades. Scalability, predictability, and replicability were the focus of those schools, because they were designed to educate a *workforce.* The effects of this design persist in environments that can be efficiently organized, monitored, and measured, priming schools to still suffer from compliance culture. Additionally, schools today are continually rated and measured via standardized testing. Compliance-based environments are built on managing adults, and they are perpetuated by a system of rewards and consequences: If you do a task on time or always say yes, you win favor with the leadership. If your students score high on tests, you get to have more choice in what subject you want to teach (reward). If your students score low, then you might receive a lower performance evaluation (consequence).

In education, we often say we value things like creating outside the box, communicating effectively, sincerity, integrity, and grit, but we continue to measure data points like test scores and grades, and we require compliant behavior. It's easier to deal with, more objective, and more quantifiable. Also, these quantifiable aspects of education fit into our outdated approaches of measuring learning: tests, grades, attendance, and behavior. Not only does measuring by test scores capture just a select few kinds of intelligence, it measures them poorly.

As a coach, you can help shift a compliance culture to a culture of collaboration, commitment, and aspiration, one that's centered on learning and working together.

What are some of the most important aspects of your role as a coach? Let's list a few:

- Becoming a supportive partner for teachers
- Setting the tone for professional learning
- Establishing trust and building relationships with teachers
- Connecting to the intrinsic motivational flows of teachers
- Being an empathetic and active listener
- Being an activator of collaboration
- Supporting the integration of technology into learning and the classroom
- Impacting student learning by supporting teachers in using effective pedagogy

You could most certainly add some more bullets to this list, but notice there is nothing about creating formative assessments or creating collaborative unit plans on it. Of course, these are well-intentioned pieces of work, but they are not aspirational aspects of our role as coaches.

Often, we talk about our role as coaches as helping teachers "get things done." When we put the actual list of tasks front and center, it communicates that we're only interested in completing the task and not concerned about the impact on student learning or the profession. This leads to the reinforcement of a compliance-based culture. We start focusing on completing the unit plan for the third six weeks instead of creating meaningful learning experiences for students. What we say and our actions and our behaviors toward our colleagues have a significant effect on our collective mindset and our collective efficacy. Below is an example of words I've heard that promote compliance versus those that promote a positive, collaborative, and productive partnership:

Compliance-driven statements	Collaborative and aspirational statements
"This is due ___"	"Given our agreed-upon goal, when would be a reasonable timeline to have this ready?"
"I need you all to close your laptops during the meeting."	"How can we all get the most out of today's meeting?"
"I need your notes before we have our debrief."	"Do you have everything you need to prepare for our debrief together?"
"I noticed you only stated the learning objective once."	"Did students understand why they were doing the activity? Is it important that they understand this? How do we ensure that happens?"
"Something seems off. What's going on?"	"I appreciate your contributions to the team, and I'm in this with you for the long haul. How do you feel about the current challenges and struggles we're facing?"

"I don't have time right now."	"You are a priority, and I want to dedicate my full attention to you. May we find a time later today or tomorrow to talk?"

When you read the statements on the left, how did they make you feel? Most of us would probably say we feel defensive or resistant reading the compliance-driven statements. They elicit an emotion that causes a reactionary response, either to resist or maybe even actively work against the speaker. The statements on the right feel much less threatening. That's because they are communicated with collaborative and productive intent. They aren't meant to force you to complete a task but to help prompt thinking, find answers to a problem, prepare for something, and treat each other with respect. These statements go very far in helping teachers see that you're not there to criticize or force compliance but to create a productive and collaborative culture.

What about the scenario where a teacher is actively working against the coach or a teacher is resisting the coaching process? Giving lots of space is my best recommendation. But work still has to occur, even in the midst of resistance. The following strategies can help de-escalate a situation with a teacher who might be angry or working through their own emotions (which is healthy):

- Create a safe space for low-stakes conversations.
- Don't bring up potential issues in front of other team members.
- Provide personal space. Don't meet in the principal's office or the teacher's classroom. You could take a walk or meet outside, weather permitting.
- Do not corner a teacher.
- Plan a time to chat. Right after school might not be the best time to talk.
- Be aware of your words. Incorporate the collaborative language from the chart above.

- Be aware of any implicit bias.
- Speak respectfully and be aware of body language.
- Be direct, don't be passive or manipulative.
- Find something you agree with.
- Be honest and transparent.
- Re-establish your role as the coach, as a partner and supporter.

◆ PROBLEM SOLVING AS VEHICLE FOR GROWTH AND NOT COMPLIANCE

As coaches, we focus much of our work on solving problems, from helping a teacher think through effective student-engagement strategies to facilitating professional development after school. In a culture of compliance, problem solving is about removing barriers so that a task can be quickly checked off a list: A teacher *has to* implement a particular technology strategy, but they're having difficulties with getting the tech to work correctly, so they want someone to please come and make it work so they can check it off the list. But problem solving should be a complex process involves collaboration, critical thinking, perseverance, patience, and the skill of working with diverse personalities at wide-ranging experience levels.

Frequently, coaches believe they support teachers by removing barriers and obstacles for their teammates. I once witnessed a coach create a yearlong proficiency map for math, because the teachers had limited time to do so themselves. Creating proficiency maps for teachers doesn't deliver a long-term solution for helping them understand the intricacies of the learning standards, what's required to learn deeply, and to make the best use of learning opportunities. The "doing the work for you" mentality erodes the coach-teacher relationship and further promotes compliance. A culture of effective and collaborative problem solving must include conversations and doing the work together, not for the sake of just removing barriers but to learn and grow together as a team.

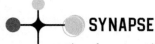

SYNAPSE

What if you've already been inadvertently promoting a compliance culture by doing the work for your teachers and you're looking at making changes? Below is an example of communication that you could use and adapt to specific situations:

> "Thank you for all the hard work and time you put into planning your lessons. I want to ensure I am supporting you to the fullest extent possible. I am reworking our scheduled meeting to create a more focused and structured time for our team to collaboratively create a common proficiency map for math. Once we work through the process of making meaning of the learning standards, we will deconstruct content standards together, create assessment items, and then plan out the scope and sequence for the rest of the year. This will allow us the opportunity to better create consistency across our team and also have more effective planning, instruction, and feedback processes. The more consistent and purposeful our collaborative meetings become, the more impactful and productive our work will be."

BALANCE OF COLLABORATION AND INDEPENDENCE

We all agree that collaboration is important. It's an important skill for students to learn so that they can be effective contributors to their community and so that they can be successful in team-oriented workplaces. For teachers, it's very important to have opportunities to collaborate, as some of our best professional development results from having quality time to plan and create with our colleagues. But we must be careful about how we're collaborating and not use every available "prep time" for collaboration or PLC (professional learning community) time. Having team members collaborate excessively and not allowing them time to think and work independently leads to bitterness, frustration, and stress. Furthermore, many team-meeting structures meant for collaboration don't actually lead to effective collaboration.

Coaches are facilitators of collaboration and therefore can ensure a creative environment that balances collaborative experiences and individual work time. Here are three suggestions that can help you create this balance:

1. Create a warm and collegial environment. With the important work required of teachers and the pressures they often face, following this principle carries more weight than ever before. Allow natural interests and hobbies to become a part of natural conversation when meeting together. Collaboration can yield very productive results, but not if people don't feel comfortable or don't enjoy being together. Do things that make people laugh. Incorporate icebreakers and games occasionally. Team-building events, group games, outdoor cookouts, birthday parties, etc. are all great ways to cultivate collegial environments.

2. Provide differentiation in the mode of your meeting and communicate goals ahead of time. Is this a meeting to share and discuss ideas or is this a meeting to workshop a new instructional approach? Is this meeting to nurture relationships in a casual environment or to solve a problem that's standing in our way? Sharing ideas and deciding on essential learning standards, tools, and instructional strategies are appropriate for meetings. But when it comes time for creation and critical thinking, don't force everyone to execute these cognitive functions in a formal environment. Provides lots of autonomy on how we get there, allowing for various approaches to solving a problem, but provide a very concrete reason on why we are meeting (for example: "This problem is keeping us from reaching our goals" or "We are huddling to create a solution").

3. Create a collaborative structure that maximizes group time and individual productivity. Some of the best ideas result from some space from others. Reflection, contemplation, and metacognition are where the pieces discussed in the meeting start to come together in new and surprising ways. During the meeting, embed some reflection time for others to make important connections between concepts discussed. More importantly, allow a day or two for team members to ruminate on ideas and create something meaningful either asynchronously or synchronously during a meeting scheduled later on.

There is currently a limit on the frequency of meetings these days. This is for good reason, as there are too many things vying for our time, and many meetings are not structured in a way to be effective and productive. But there are two types of meetings that should never get canceled: PLC/team meetings and one-on-one sync-ups.

PLC/team meetings are crucial to the success of planning for grade-level and/or content-level success of students learning in your building. There will always be work to get done: establishing essential learning standards, creating formative assessments, shopping for new creative instructional strategies, creating intervention and enrichment resources, unit planning, etc. These are all functions of the school-wide learning processes that must be carried out in teams. These meetings should happen at least once a week. Canceling just one team meeting can lead to confusion, resentment, a decrease in accountability, and a loss in momentum.

One-on-one meetings are also crucial for the success of the coach-teacher relationship. It's also essential to the coach-principal relationship. These one-on-ones are opportunities to provide helpful feedback to teachers or gather crucial feedback from teachers. These meetings allow teachers a platform to discuss emotions they're feeling about something, a problem they're grappling with, or a shining moment in their week. You can see how canceling this kind of meeting is detrimental to your coach-teacher relationship. Many issues can fester into larger problems if not addressed. A regular cadence of one-on-ones gives teachers a consistent structure to share roadblocks, challenges, opportunities, ideas, and solutions.

Yes, you have classrooms to get into, PD sessions to plan, a training at the district office, an afterschool tutoring session you're facilitating for students, and so many more things on your plate. But when school seems the busiest, it's also the most stressful, which means your one-on-one meetings have the opportunity to have the biggest impact, even if it means just listening to a teacher share what's on their mind or lending a helping hand. You are never too busy for these meetings, because if you're doing them right, you've prioritized them.

What if you don't have anything to discuss or talk about? If that's the case, reevaluate how you're structuring your one-on-one meetings. Are you asking questions about a teacher's goals? What risks they're taking? What they need from you? What ideas they'd like to try out?

◆ SOCIAL CONTAGION

You're at a restaurant, and the friends you're with order a dessert. You weren't going to order one, but now you have to order one. Or the teacher down the hall is now using a new tech tool, and now we're curious and want to try it out. Behavioral contagion or social contagion is a type of social influence. It refers to the propensity for a person to copy behaviors of others who are either in the vicinity or whom they have been exposed to. We often "catch" certain behaviors without even realizing it. You might realize one day you're doing something because the person you're living with is doing it. Your spouse or partner is more direct in their conflict-resolution style, and now you're noticing you're more direct in tense situations. This is a natural part of human behavior.

It's also something to note as you're thinking about the culture of your team meetings or just the professional culture that exists in your school. Think about a team in your building that's known for their positive attitude and jovial demeanor. There are probably one or two teachers on this team that are energetic and consistently display a high mood and therefore have an impact on the team. Now think about a team that consistently pushes back or has a negative attitude. As with the more positive team, the more negative behaviors probably result from one or two teachers who are continually expressing a negative attitude and casting a lower mood onto the team.

As a coach, it's not your job to change or fix someone's mood or their emotions. That's not really anyone's job.

SYNAPSE

You're looking at supporting a team to make them more functional and productive. There are a few supportive posturing strategies you can employ:

- Take responsibility for your mood. If someone walks into a meeting with a low mood, don't take responsibility for their mood, as if the meeting caused it. There is something else going on in their world, and as much as we might want to put our game face on, our emotions have an effect on how we behave at work.

- Be a listening ear. Ask how things are going and genuinely listen.

- After listening, determine if this person needs empathy or a solution. If you're not able to discern, ask the person.

- Show compassion for someone's situation.

Over time, showing support and being a listening ear will pay off for the culture of the team. It's also important to point back to the bigger picture. We're in a team because we're working to ensure student learning. Sometimes we can get buried in the weeds and we need a gentle reminder of what our purpose is.

Your culture-connection pathway is made up of the many decisions and processes made everyday: the language you use, how and why you give feedback, avoiding compliance, balancing collaboration and independence, and using positive social contagion. Culture is continually evolving, minute by minute, person by person, decision by decision. This culture pathway cannot be replaced or transferred, it can only evolve and shift. As the coach, you have a role to play in evolving this pathway. It starts with your leadership and your commitment to connection.

PATHWAY OF COMMUNICATION

BECOMING A BETTER LISTENER

Being an effective communicator hinges entirely upon being a good listener and a good asker of questions. Good listening and inquiring skills, whether innate or garnered through years of patient and cultivated experience, include the capacity to be unruffled and avoid defensiveness ("Argh!") with information that may challenge certain deeply held assumptions. Good listeners are straightforward, unfazed, and patient—immune to the chaos others often create. They have built a vast repository of equanimity, because they are comfortable with temporary bewilderment and are able to navigate disequilibrium as a part of learning.

The best coaches encourage teachers to share their voices, spread their ideas, and develop their communication skills through presenting and facilitating professional development. However, in order to fully support teachers, we must develop the conditions in which their voices can make an impact.

◆ *PERSUASION*

I had a new idea for a lesson. It was interactive and chock-full of strategies I hadn't tried before, and I was excited about implementing it. I worked on a team that developed lessons together, so we all had previously agreed-upon norms for how we would work together. We would vet each other's lessons, provide feedback to each other, practice strategies, and then agree to implement them.

There was one team member in particular who was always hard to convince of new ideas. He had a traditional approach to teaching. He became predictable in his resistance. "We can't do that this way because..." I almost always anticipated his pushback. One day, I saw him using a new strategy and I asked him about it. The strategy he had tried was something he'd discovered, thought through, and implemented on his own. I realized he wasn't being set in his ways, he just needed time to process new ideas in a way that made sense to him. Our way of sharing new ideas in a group setting was causing him to have a reactive posture of "no." He needed some semblance of control.

So, I tried a new approach. Before our next team meeting, I met with him and said, "I have a new lesson I'd like to present to the group. I think it makes sense, but I'm sure there are things I'm not thinking of. If I share this with you first, could you think about it for a day or two and then give me feedback before I share with the rest of the group?" He seemed surprised, but then he smiled. My presenting this idea to him this way showed I valued his wisdom and experience. It communicated that I didn't just want him to go along with my idea, I genuinely wanted his opinion. It gave him time to process my idea the way he felt most comfortable, not out in front of the group. He came back to me the very next day, very positive, and with just a couple of notes. He even took some ownership and led the meeting with me the next day, sharing the new strategy as if it were something he was already a part of. It wasn't my idea or the fact that it was a new idea that mattered—it was my approach that mattered.

How many times have we labeled someone as "old school" or "negative" because they pushed back on our new ideas, not realizing it was the approach we were using that upset them? The next time you encounter this kind of resistance, reflect on your approach. Are you asking people to jump onboard with new ideas immediately? Are there opportunities to involve others in ways that align more to their implementation style? Can you champion the needs of others in your ideas before presenting to the larger group?

Asking the opinion of a hesitant or resistant team member can do wonders for more productive collaboration. An "objective" method for evaluating best practices might help everyone feel like they can get on the same page more easily—including those who are resistant to change. If there is a test the group can agree on for evaluation and a strategy passes that test, it's easier to achieve consensus.

Philosopher Carl Sagan (1995) developed a "baloney detection kit," a set of cognitive tools and techniques that fortify the mind against the invasion of falsehoods and "fake news." The tools involve these nine tips:

1. Wherever possible there must be independent confirmation of the "facts."

2. Encourage substantive debate on the evidence by knowledgeable proponents of all points of view.

3. Arguments from authority carry little weight—"authorities" have made mistakes in the past. They will do so again in the future. Perhaps a better way to say it is that in science there are no authorities; at most, there are experts.

4. Spin more than one hypothesis. If there's something to be explained, think of all the different ways in which it could be explained. Then think of tests by which you might systematically disprove each of the alternatives. What survives, the hypothesis that resists disproof in this Darwinian selection among "multiple working hypotheses," has a much better

chance of being the right answer than if you had simply run with the first idea that caught your fancy.

5. Try not to get overly attached to a hypothesis just because it's yours. It's only a way station in the pursuit of knowledge. Ask yourself why you like the idea. Compare it fairly with the alternatives. See if you can find reasons for rejecting it. If you don't, others will.

6. Quantify. If whatever it is you're explaining has some measure, some numerical quantity attached to it, you'll be much better able to discriminate among competing hypotheses. What is vague and qualitative is open to many explanations. Of course there are truths to be sought in the many qualitative issues we are obliged to confront, but finding them is more challenging.

7. If there's a chain of argument, every link in the chain must work (including the premise)—not just most of them.

8. Occam's Razor. This convenient rule of thumb urges us when faced with two hypotheses that explain the data equally well to choose the simpler.

9. Always ask whether the hypothesis can be, at least in principle, falsified. Propositions that are untestable, unfalsifiable, are not worth much. You must be able to check assertions out. Other skeptics must be given the chance to follow your reasoning, to duplicate your experiments and see if they get the same result.

I think these tips can be helpful as you navigate the many strategies or "best practices" that come your way. A very important note here: these tips are to equip you in your own individual evaluation of information flooding you. I am not suggesting you take these tips and go start debates with colleagues. Using baloney detection will help produce group consensus with less conflict, but using this method to debate the suggestions of others without the group agreeing on the Sagan method would just be asking for trouble. As we discussed earlier, sharing all of your arguments and data points with someone who is struggling to get the group to agree is just going to make them more vehemently against your position.

It's important that we are able to evaluate concepts and information as we make meaning of the world. But tread with care here. We tend to assign an evaluation to someone's opinion or belief and might say, "I am right" and "you are wrong" or "that's ignorant" or "that's good thinking." Instead of assigning a label, what if we instead approached it another way? "What would have to be true about the world in order for that idea to be a good one?" For example, what would have to be true about student learning for an assignment with copious amounts of practice problems to be a good idea?

So, what is the answer here? It's about being able to evaluate ideas but also showing empathy as we do so. Showing empathy doesn't mean we are accepting someone's point of view. It means we're moving toward understanding the context for their point of view. It's also important that we're all moving in the same direction. We all want our world to be a better place, and we want our students to learn and succeed at the highest levels. We have this in common. Let this common ground be a foundation for empathy. Being aware of your reactions and biases while being willing to listen and to change your mind will bring you far in your empathy journey.

BUILDING EMPATHY

Empathy is most often described as imagining what it's like to be in someone else's shoes. The first mistake people make with empathy is that tricky word "imagine." Often, what we imagine is a complete guess, because we have no clue what it's like to be in someone else's shoes. We have our own past experiences we can conjure up, but, at best, we can tangentially compare our experiences with those of someone else. Empathy begins and ends with listening. That means we must stop guessing or assuming we know what it's like to experience what someone else is experiencing and actually take the time to ask. Ask, and then listen.

Why is empathy important in the coach-teacher role? After all, we're not therapists or counselors, asking teachers to lie on the coach in our office and share all the things that are bringing them down. That's a very narrow view of empathy. But we are in a role that affords us the opportunity to influence teacher decision-making in a positive way. To empathize with someone is to actively pursue an understanding of how they view the world. When someone shares something you believe is outlandish, how do you react? You probably experience a very visceral, instantaneous reaction. Let's say that you believe homework isn't an effective strategy for student learning. And then a colleague says, "I am giving my students a lot of practice problems over the winter break because they will fall behind if I don't." Your initial reaction is probably, "They're wrong! That's not right! They're damaging student learning! Noooo!" Or something like that. This response is known as the backfire effect. Psychologist David McRaney (2013) says this about the backfire effect:

> Once something is added to your collection of beliefs, you protect it from harm. You do this instinctively and unconsciously when confronted with attitude-inconsistent information. Just as confirmation bias shields you when you actively seek information, the backfire effect defends you when the information seeks you, when it blindsides you. Coming or going, you stick to your beliefs instead of questioning them. When someone tries to correct you, tries to dilute your misconceptions, it backfires and strengthens those misconceptions instead. Over time, the backfire effect makes you less skeptical of those things that allow you to continue seeing your beliefs and attitudes as true and proper.

There is neurological research to illuminate why we behave this way.

And what do we do when someone challenges a deep-seated belief? We start finding information, facts, and quotes to back up our belief. Then the other person digs in their heels even more. How often does someone say, "Oh, thank you for that proof. I have now changed my mind because of your compelling argument." That just doesn't happen; the opposite tends to happen, in fact. The other person then finds more quotes and articles to match their position, making them stauncher in their original belief system. Empathy is a way to overcome the backfire effect. This communication technique helps build consensus between you and the teacher. Let's discuss a pragmatic way to show a teacher that you're truly embodying empathy.

◆ PIVOTAL QUESTION: DO YOU WANT A SOLUTION OR EMPATHY?

We've all encountered a day when we've just been through it. Maybe it was a day when you felt like you were just putting out fires all day. At the end of the day, you might just want to vent all your emotions. When I encounter something difficult in my day, I will sometimes want to express my emotions to my husband, Herbie. Sometimes I come to him with a problem that I'd like his perspective on so that I can reason through the best possible solution. But not always. You've probably encountered those times, when you just want to vent your emotions to a spouse, partner, friend, or family member, and you don't want a solution—you just need empathy. You want someone there to listen to you, empathize with your situation, and be on your side. That is what you need in the moment, not a solution.

Herbie and I have a phrase that we use with each other so that we can best meet each other's needs: Do you want a solution or just empathy? Often, we can just tell it's empathy. But sometimes we might have a potential solution when the other person doesn't want one. Resist the temptation to share your advice or solution to the problem. If you're not sure what they need, just ask: Do you need empathy or a solution? Maybe it's both.

When a teacher is sharing with a coach, the coach experiences what it's like to see the world from the teacher's perspective. This experience of feeling and understanding is empathy. Empathy leads to better decision-making, considering others' perspectives, and respect for different worldviews. Empathy leads to more effective collaboration and working toward common goals with trust and open, honest communication.

Coaches often hear that the best way to connect with fellow teachers is to empathize. But how can educators better encourage empathy between themselves, their students, and other groups of students?

First, let's acknowledge that it can be challenging to reach a deep sense of empathy, especially if one does not have similar experiences to those being expressed. Showing true empathy requires exploring why the other person feels or experiences the world in their particular way. Empathy isn't created by the coach guessing the teacher's intent or imagining what it's like to be in someone else's shoes. In fact, empathy starts when listeners stop guessing at what's on the mind of teachers and peers and instead learn to actively listen.

Coaches can express empathy toward their colleagues by asking teachers to share their thinking. When a teacher shares, they are expressing their understanding on an intellectual level as well as revealing how they think and feel about a particular experience or concept. When teacher thinking is effectively shared and heard, coaches and fellow teachers are equipped with the information needed to join in on reacting to that perspective.

◆ FOUR STEPS TO BUILDING EMPATHY BETWEEN COACH AND TEACHER

There are four simple steps coaches can employ to encourage active listening and build empathy among their colleagues:

1. Listen to the perspective the teacher is sharing.

2. Paraphrase what the teacher just shared. The coach summarizes the teacher's message by restating the big idea and reflecting on the feelings they felt when hearing the story. "So, I heard you saying..." or "This is what I understand to be your emotion about..."

3. Receive confirmation from the teacher that you have perceived their perspective the way they intended.

4. Allow the teacher to reflect upon the coach's perspectives. That might sound like "I felt like I had something important to share when you gave cues that you were listening to me" or "I felt valued when you were focused on listening to my story."

Active listening allows both the teacher and the coach to develop a depth of understanding and provides a window into the storyteller's values, levels of thinking, emotions, and presuppositions behind their experiences. Building deeper learning through meaningful experiences requires sensitivity, empathy, self-awareness, social awareness, and active listening. When educators work together in environments with high empathy, collaboration and learning can be transformative.

 SYNAPSE

You can practice empathy toward your colleagues by asking them to share their thinking. It could be about an upcoming initiative, the last PD session they attended, or a new strategy that was introduced to them during the coaching cycle. Practice active listening when they're talking: positive and attentive body language, paraphrasing, confirming an accurate perception, and encouraging them to reflect further. You will not only build your listening skills but you will also gain invaluable insight.

This template is a good way to document and keep track of your conversations. It's best not to fill this out during the conversation (because you're listening), but immediately after.

Conversation Reflection Template

Date:_____

Conversation with: _____

Topic of conversation:

Do you have an accurate perception of their thinking?
Why or why not?

What I want to ask them for the next conversation:

ENTHUSIASM

You know those days? When we're on our way to school and we suddenly find ourselves startled by the beauty of the sunrise or experience joyful enthusiasm for the opportunity to teach eager minds and help students be their best selves? This doesn't happen by accident. It's only when we stop trying to be productive and busy all the time that we are able to see the beauty around us. Enthusiasm is deeply tied to our purpose but gets buried by busyness and the routine of school structure. Enthusiasm is not only helpful for promoting a positive culture; it is also a tactical communication strategy. Coaches can be instrumental in cultivating enthusiasm in the school community. You can model self-care as you also build these strategies into team meetings and throughout the school day.

One of the ways you can build a positive school culture of communication is in the kind of enthusiasm you have for your fellow colleagues and students. As teachers, we have a caring interest in our students and the work we're doing. Some days we find ourselves struggling not to compare ourselves with others, and we will either inflate our own egos by diminishing the worth of someone else or we will focus on someone else's achievements to our detriment. This kind of vanity can lead to an unproductive and unhealthy competitiveness. One of the best antidotes for this is to embrace the notion that others are pulling for you. You'll naturally reciprocate this enthusiasm to others.

Only you are responsible for your own enthusiasm and happiness. It is so easy to get trapped by negativity.

I have had times in my professional life where the tasks were insurmountable, the to-do lists didn't have an end in sight, a new state assessment was required, new standards had to be implemented, and stakes had never seemed higher.

If only I didn't have twenty parent phone calls to return, I could spend more time in classrooms.

If only I didn't have one hundred brand-new emails in my inbox, I could focus on team-meeting facilitation.

We know from experience the grass isn't always greener and that once we do get to the other side, we find that someone else's field is even greener. But it's not the acquisition of something new that will make you happy. There will always be greener grass.

You, and only you, should be responsible for your own happiness.

◆ QANTAS FLIGHT 32

Have you ever panicked and did or said something you later regretted? Or you were stressed, and became so hyperfocused on the present, you lost sight of your priorities? Situations can dilute your ability to communicate effectively if we don't have a clear focus on our priorities.

It was a beautiful morning in Singapore as Qantas Airways Flight 32 took off and began its journey to Sydney. A few minutes after take-off, the pilot, Richard de Crespigny, turned on the plane's autopilot. Shortly after, the pilots heard a boom. Then there was another, even louder crash, followed by what sounded like thousands of marbles being thrown against the hull. Alarms started popping up on the computer display. Engine two was on fire. Engine three was damaged. There was no data at all for engines one and four. The fuel pumps were failing. The hydraulics, pneumatics, and electrical systems were essentially inoperative. Fuel was leaking from the left wing. What happened would later be described as one of the worst midair mechanical disasters in modern aviation.

There were so many broken systems on this plane that as soon as one alarm was put out, more alarms would start. Richard de Crespigny realized he was falling into a cognitive tunnel— when the brain is so overwhelmed, it can only focus on the most observable stimuli.

As the pilot was tunneling, he came to a point where he thought, "What's the most important thing to do here?" Instead of responding, he began thinking. In the middle of the alarms, he closed his eyes and realized, "I am falling into a cognitive tunnel. I need to feel in control. If I'm in control, I'll make better choices."

The first airplane de Crespigny had ever flown was a Cessna, a single engine, almost entirely noncomputerized plane that many novice pilots learn on. "What if," de Crespigny thought to himself, "I imagine this plane as a Cessna? What would I do then?"

He ended up landing the plane without any incidents. His was able to make the right choices when he thought about treating the plane as if it were a Cessna. Instead of uncontrollably reacting, he decided how to behave.

It is important that we build a scaffold (a pathway) for the stimuli that constantly bombards us. This intentionally created pathway helps us choose where to channel our thinking so we can make decisions rather than just react. Think for a moment about the pressures you face each day. Let's say you are stressed out with a lot of things going and you also happen to be in a meeting with your principal. The principal suddenly asks you for an opinion. Your mind is likely to snap from distraction to reaction—and if you're not careful, a cognitive tunnel might prompt you to say something you don't mean. If you are juggling multiple conversations and tasks at once and an important email arrives, reactive thinking can cause you to type a reply before you've really thought out what you want to say.

Doing a better job of communicating begins with knowing what your priorities are and paying attention to what really matters. As a coach, you will get a constant bombardment of emails, requests, conversations, and interruptions every day. Know what to focus on and what to ignore, and get into the habit of telling yourself what your purpose is.

This same purpose-filled passion fueling our enthusiasm should unfold in our coaching journey. And when we are struggling, stressed, or tunneling, we should ask ourselves the same questions:

- What is it about coaching that you love?
- What specific part about the process of coaching do you love?
- What parts of coaching, leading, and teaching make you question why you do it?
- What experiences have energized you or made your soul happy?
- How do you create a mindset that sustains your own happiness?

These questions should get you back to the place where it all started for you: your love of teaching and learning. This reflection allows you to rediscover what first drew you into education. We must rediscover our love—our enthusiasm—for coaching. Notice I chose the word "rediscover." You were never really without your passion. But we all need reminding of that purpose that drives our passion and enthusiasm. We can remember and reconnect with our enthusiasm by better understanding ourselves, discovering what it was about influential educators and leaders in our lives that inspired us, emulating those qualities, and creating professional learning opportunities for ourselves, our students, our colleagues, and our communities that not only equip and support but also renew our sense of heart for teaching.

Communicating with enthusiasm isn't some false perspective you adopt to respond positively in the midst of problems. Enthusiasm is a natural outflow of the disposition of purpose you've realized. You do the work to tap into this purpose. An important component of being responsible for our own enthusiasm and promoting empathy is creating intentional time for self-care.

You can't show empathy to someone else if you don't show it to yourself first. As educators, our stress can become overwhelming. Ensuring that our students have a nurturing and positive environment, being responsive to parents and fellow colleagues, creative and innovative instructional design, collaborative planning, etc.—it's no wonder why educators are among the most valued and overworked professionals. We cannot be our best selves when we have lost ourselves in the work. The secret to being the best coach and leader you can be is to take care of yourself and your own happiness first.

Below are some simple but powerful things you can do to be your best self at work and at home:

- Schedule self-care (open your Google Calendar right now and add it!).
- Be more YOU (whoever you are, embrace YOU and then be more YOU).
- Acknowledge your strengths.
- Protect your time.
- Prioritize your time.
- Nurture your inner life.
- Seek solitude (yes, even extroverts need alone time).
- Read for pleasure (you don't always have to read education books).
- Be outside (take strolls, hike, bike, etc.).
- Turn off your notifications (they aren't going anywhere—you won't miss a thing).

A friend and mentor also told me to "pull my own happiness wagon." This saying resonates with me each and every day. I actively strive to live by this idea. My happiness doesn't depend on other people or external forces but solely on my attitude and choices. As a coach, you're pulling your own enthusiasm wagon. And when you pull your own wagon, you see good everywhere. You are able to communicate your enthusiasm to those you lead and contribute to a healthier school culture.

SYNAPSE

When you feel overly stressed or like you're in a rut, return to these questions to re-spark your enthusiasm for coaching:

- What is it about coaching that you love?
- What part about the process of coaching do you love?
- What parts of coaching, leading, and teaching make you question why you do it?
- What experiences have energized you or made your soul happy?
- How do you create a mindset that embodies creating your own happiness?

PATHWAY OF EMOTIONAL INTELLIGENCE

EMOTIONAL INTELLIGENCE

Psychology has significant insight into how adults work with each other, especially in the school setting. Emotional intelligence (EI), for example, affects how we manage our behavior, communicate in social situations, and interact with others. Research has also shown that it is the number-one predictor of performance. Therefore we can make connections that demonstrate the relationship between high EI and effective instructional coaching relationships.

The relationship between a coach and the school has an impact on emotional intelligence. The manifestation of this impact is seen in the kinds of emotions we chose to display or the particular way we feel toward our work. There have been many attempts for schools to help educators love their work so that they can be more intrinsically motivated. School leaders have to be careful about this, so as not to seem to be manipulating the emotions of educators to get short-term compliance.

In this chapter we will discuss the components that connect together to form the EI pathway: self-awareness, finding your focus, and creating common understanding.

◆ SELF-AWARENESS

An important component of EI is self-awareness. We often go through the school day reacting and acting, never really thinking about how or why we respond the way we do.

SYNAPSE

We can develop self-awareness by asking questions to get to the crux of how and why we respond the way we do. Carve out thirty minutes of time and answer the following questions:

For All Educators:

- How does my mindset affect my effort in working with others?
- How does my mindset affect others?
- Do I tend to make decisions slowly or quickly?
- How does my mood affect my thoughts and decision-making?
- Do I tend to focus on the positive or negative traits of others?
- What dispositions in others bother me? Why?
- Do I find it difficult to admit when I'm wrong? Why or why not?

Specifically for Coaches:

- How does my mindset cause me to see coaching differently?
- How does my mindset change the cycle of thinking and learning?
- How does my mindset connect coaching experiences, actions, and behaviors?
- How can I better ask questions to help coaching become more meaningful?
- How does my coaching and communication influence teachers' pedagogy in meaningful ways?
- How does my role cause teachers to see the classroom differently?
- How does the struggle in the teaching profession deepen my own thinking about instruction and learning?

Specifically for Teachers:

- How does my mindset cause me to see my classroom differently?
- How does my mindset cause me to see my administration and colleagues differently?
- How does my mindset change the cycle of thinking and learning?
- How does my mindset connect teaching experiences, actions, and behaviors?

- How can I better ask questions to help teaching become more personally meaningful?
- How does my teaching and communication influence my students' learning in meaningful ways?
- How does my behavior influence the way my students see the classroom?
- How does the struggle in the teaching profession deepen my own thinking about instruction and learning?

The answers to these questions can give great insight into your own self-awareness. It's also helpful to provide this list of questions to teachers so they can go through a similar reflective process. Once you've built a genuine trust with your teachers, you can have one-on-one meetings to get some insight into how they answered these questions. This helps you understand how they view themselves and how they view the world. We also know that experiences over time will change personal beliefs, attitudes, and influences. With a deeper understanding of our own self-awareness and a greater awareness of others, we will better plan for collaborative sessions focused on creativity and innovation.

Consider this example:

Let's say Teacher A embraces the chaos in our educational institutions and has the flexibility, spontaneity, and systems thinking to navigate each day.

Teacher B is doing everything they can to stay afloat, because the challenges and stresses of each day are overwhelming.

Teacher A and Teacher B have very different ways of seeing the world. When a change initiative is presented to a team, Teacher A will accept this as a part of their daily work. Teacher A will make the necessary tweaks to effectively implement this change. Teacher B will probably resist and, as a result, will do the bare minimum regarding the new change or just implement it on a surface level out of a fear of being reprimanded. Teacher B is hanging on by a thread, and wonders how in the world they will find the energy or time to even make this change.

Do you see how the same change initiative affects people in very different ways? Not only is it important that a coach recognize these different circumstances, viewpoints, and corresponding reactions, it's important that Teacher A and Teacher B can reflect on their responses to the self-awareness questions and see how their individual perspectives influence how they'll view and implement change. The questions can help guide conversations around teachers' own self-awareness and connected emotional intelligence.

FINDING YOUR FOCUS

Have you ever walked into a classroom to make an observation and been overwhelmed by what you saw? Teachers make thousands of decisions every day that impact students and their learning in both positive and negative ways. The number of decisions I've seen teachers make over the course of a brief observation is astounding. For example, we might observe the following decisions:

- Teaching whole group or small group
- Introducing content through lecture or reading
- Having students work independently, in partners, or groups
- Whether or not to pose questions, which questions to ask, who answers, and how those questions will be answered
- Whether or not to write something on the board or show an image and what that might be
- What kind of feedback students receive, when they get it, and how it's delivered
- How to correct a behavior or an error

There is so much to observe when you are in a classroom, so how do you decide what might be the focus of the coaching conversation to have with that teacher? Additionally, what if a teacher says your observations are subjective and not factual? Truthfully, most of your thoughts about what is happening in the classroom are not factual but evaluations and judgments entwined with emotions, some positive and helpful, some negative and counterproductive. It's important we are aware of how our emotions are impacting our observations. This is a part of evaluating our own emotional intelligence.

◆ SCHOOL-WIDE INSTRUCTIONAL GOALS AND ALIGNMENT

When you visit classrooms, what are the primary things you look for? We often call them look-fors. Take a moment and write them down.

Next question: do your teachers know what these look-fors are? Is there clarity and transparency regarding them? If not, we've already created a misalignment of goals and perceptions.

Coaching works best when there is also alignment and clarity in the system regarding the instructional changes we are all trying to make in order to dramatically improve student learning. What does that mean in practice? It means that the following would be in place:

1. Agreed-upon school-wide instructional goals based on data
2. Clear expectations that we will all be working on the goals
3. Collaborative professional learning opportunities focused on those instructional goals
4. Professional learning communities (PLCs) planning together with those goals in mind
5. Classroom observations focused on the instructional goals
6. Opportunities to practice and receive feedback focused on the goals
7. Coaching and support aligned to the goals
8. A system to hold each other accountable to meeting the goals
9. A data-collection system to determine whether we're meeting the goals and making the instructional shifts
10. A data-collection system to determine whether student learning is improving as the instructional shifts are made

If you are a coach working in a school or a system that has this kind of alignment, it makes your job easier. For example, if student engagement is a school-wide focus, there are goals around it, collaborative learning on what it is, and ways to strengthen it in a classroom, etc. You and the teacher have a common understanding of your purpose in making classroom observations and what the focus of your conversation will be when you engage in coaching dialogues.

Lack of clarity and focus creates disorder and an unproductive collaborative relationship. How can you feel like you're getting somewhere if the goal posts seem to be constantly moving? If one week you visit a teacher's classroom and have a coaching conversation about higher-order thinking, the next week you give feedback on explicitly explaining and modeling a concept, and one week later you focus on a strategy for student engagement, your coaching is all over the map. You send a message that you're flying by the seat of your pants as opposed to providing coaching and support tied to an agreed-upon plan with the teacher aligned to the instructional goals. Goals, a plan, and opportunities for practice and focused feedback are essential for your coaching to have a positive impact on learning and growth.

Below is a sample set of instructional items that a system/school may be focused on:

- Alignment to standards at the right level of complexity for the grade level
- Level of complexity of the student task
- Who does the thinking work?
- Active student engagement for all
- Appropriate levels of scaffolding
- Differentiated support
- Equity

It is important to note that if you are going to set goals around the development of instructional practices, they need to be based on data, tied to student-learning outcomes, and ideally agreed upon by grade level or department. Having a set of agreed-upon practices to work on together helps narrow the focus for a coach when observing instruction and planning coaching conversations. It also helps eliminate surprises and promote transparency, because there is common agreement around the instructional practices the team is working on together to improve student learning. When teachers feel like their goals are aligned with the coach's goals, they feel seen, heard, acknowledged, and cared for by their leadership, which improves their performance.

◆ DEVELOPING COMMON UNDERSTANDING

Emotionally intelligent teachers are able to confidently face stressful situations and are able to navigate tumultuous circumstances and still positively impact student learning and well-being. Teachers that have built high EI are able to see the big picture as well as how their daily choices impact student-learning outcomes and student engagement. One of the ways you can cultivate EI practices with teachers is to discuss and construct common understandings about teaching practices and the impacts on learning.

In my workshops, sometimes I show a video clip of a teacher teaching a lesson to their students. I ask coaches to watch the video clip and take notes about what they observe. Since student engagement is one of the biggest focuses for coaches and teachers, I ask the participants to keep two questions in mind as they observe:

1. How were all students engaged?
2. What evidence shows the impact of student learning?

SYNAPSE

When you're doing a walkthrough or informal observation, use this simple recording form:

Activity/Task	1) How were all students engaged?	2) What evidence shows the impact of student learning?

When the video is over, before I ask them to share their observation notes with others, I ask everyone the same question and ask them to respond by making a "fist to five" to show the level of engagement of students. A fist means zero engagement, and five fingers means a completely student-centered environment with higher-order thinking and rich engagement. I have shown this video many times to many different audiences, and inevitably, in a room full of educators who believe engaging students is a critical component of effective teaching, about half the room believes the students in the video to be engaged at a level 2 and the other half believes them to be at a level 4. That's a wide variance. This isn't an attempt at a research study, but it emphasizes the value of coming to a common understanding about what student engagement looks like. Many times it comes to not having an understood, concise, and commonly held definition of what student engagement means and how we know it when we see it in a classroom.

This exercise shows a microcosm of what happens in schools and classrooms across the country. As educators, we all know and use the buzzwords, but unless we have studied concepts like what it means for students to be engaged in the learning together as a team, our understanding of what engagement is and how it manifests itself in the classroom can and will be different from one person to the next. And that's a recipe for disaster as a coach.

Continuing with the student engagement example, if I just observed a classroom where I believed that the students were not engaged in the learning because of my own personal criteria for high student engagement, and the teacher believes they were engaged based on their working definition and understanding, we have a problem. This problem could potentially erode trust, diminish the teacher's perception of coaches, and call into question whether or not we can adequately support them.

One of the most important things a system, school, team, or coaching partnership can do after setting an instructional goal is to develop a collective understanding of what that pedagogical practice is based on—what the research says about it—as opposed to what we simply think it means. If you are working on a pedagogical practice together, you should be learning about that practice together. That will allow you, your team, and your coaching partner to all have the same understanding of what the practice is and what it isn't. It will also allow you to work together on the most powerful ways to use that practice in the classroom in order to have the biggest impact on student learning.

As I discussed earlier, a common misperception that teachers have about coaches is that the coach is trying to "fix them." Making it a priority to learn about a pedagogical practice together and working together to develop a common understanding of its impact on student learning is a great way to help remedy that perception. Coaching is about creating a collaborative culture of learning and growing in our craft. Grounding our work in learning and improving emotional intelligence together is a critical step to helping develop that culture.

SYNAPSE

An effective way of generating common look-fors is to agree upon what evidence shows high levels of student engagement. With your teacher teams, engage in a collaborative workshop where you generate ideas about what student engagement looks like, feels like, and sounds like. From this activity, you'll be able to generate a list that will become your look-fors.

Student Engagement		
Looks Like	Sounds Like	Feels Like

EMOTIONAL AGILITY

Because coaches are leaders, they will encounter tough situations that will activate inner emotions and experiences. We can develop emotional agility when we approach our inner experiences in a mindful, value-driven, and productive way. In our complex, fast changing school environments, this ability to manage one's thoughts and feelings is essential to coaching success. Many times, we want to block out difficult thoughts and emotions, because they aren't pleasant. Effective leaders are mindful of their inner experiences but not caught in them. They know how to free up their internal resources and commit to actions that align with their values.

There is no quick fix to developing emotional agility. But over time, coaches who become increasingly adept at it are the ones most likely to thrive. Real and lasting change results from the simple everyday actions and the small steps a teacher takes in the classroom to maximize student learning as well as the simple everyday support from an effective coach. Emotional agility is a marathon, not a sprint.

School-wide transformation is not only an all-hands-on-deck effort; it's a decision for each individual to do their own reflective work.

This requires patience and emotional maturity. Emotional maturity begins with the strength to sense and admit our own irrational and impulsive behavior without defensiveness. If we are truly self-aware, we are regularly willing to admit to embarrassment, laugh at our mistakes, and then grow from the insight we gain. I was working as the education supervisor at the NASA Johnson Space Center in Houston, Texas. I had been a high school science teacher, had worked at NASA developing and teaching STEM lessons, and moved to managing education teams there. I was ready for the next step in my journey: being a principal at a public elementary school. I had enrolled in grad school while teaching and working at NASA and graduated with my masters in administration.

I not only wanted to be a principal, I was looking for a place to apply my experiences at NASA and in STEM. There was a school outside of Nashville, Tennessee, that was in the process of becoming a STEM magnet school and was looking for an assistant principal. I applied, and a few days later, I had an interview with district administration and the building principal. It went well and they offered me the position.

I was so excited! Not only did I have an opportunity to provide leadership and support to educators, I was in the unique position of helping to transform a traditionally zoned school to a STEM magnet school. My first few months as a new assistant principal were quite surreal—and also challenging. I was very young, not even thirty years old. I also had a very youthful face, so I felt I had to go the extra mile to be perceived as wise and experienced. I ensured my "Dr." title was used. I was very careful not to use language that would seem casual or glib. I took my job very seriously, but I worried I was taking myself too seriously.

Sometimes even when parents would meet me at the school, they would joke about me looking like a student. One day, I decided to make a joke out of it: "Yeah, I'm so glad I got my driver's license yesterday so that I could come to work." We all had a great laugh. That laughter was disarming and immediately changed the tone of my meetings. The temperature got warmer. From that moment on, I realized that humility, vulnerability, and humor are great cornerstones of my leadership style. Having the flexibility to make fun of yourself is a mark of a confident and secure leader. It is also a sign of emotional maturity.

Susan David, PhD, a renowned psychologist and author of *Emotional Agility* (2016), says that agility is a process that enables us to navigate life's twists and turns with acceptance, clear-sightedness, and an open mind. Not only is this great advice for any human, but it can help us specifically with how we view the coaching role. Dr. David shares a helpful analogy to frame how we should view our emotions and thoughts: You see yourself as the chessboard, filled with possibilities, rather than as any one piece on the board confined to certain pre-ordained moves. We often feel an emotion and immediately associate a narrative with it: "I feel cranky because..." or "I am happy because..." Sometimes, we might even try to mask an emotion by telling ourselves we should just find the silver lining in the midst of a challenge or to be happy anyway because of what's good around us.

It's important to put space between the stimuli of an emotion and our reaction to it. Emotions are transient and a part of the human condition. It's okay to feel all emotions. Coaches should allow teachers to vent without labeling them as negative. When teachers are allowed to feel all their emotions, problem solving and innovation flourish in schools. Coaches have a very important role in transforming school culture: allowing teachers the freedom to experience emotions that are usually labeled as negative. Anger, fear, and sadness are part of the human experience, and will come out eventually in coach-teacher interactions. What can you do as a coach?

- Be present
- Don't tell someone how to feel
- Ask questions
- Truly listen
- Be empathetic

Eventually the emotion will pass, but do you know what will stay? You will be remembered for how you reacted and how supportive you were when the other person was experiencing those emotions. Being supportive and empathetic does wonders for culture, collaboration, and communication in a building. And you as the coach are poised to be a catalyst for change.

Change is an opportunity to make an impact on the world, to forge a new pathway in the coaching connectome. In my experience, it can be a long journey for some people on the team to see the upside of change. The reality is they often get overwhelmed by it. We all do at some point when faced with change. We all have heard colleagues confess that they were overwhelmed and didn't think they could "do it." As a leader who genuinely cares about people and believes wholeheartedly in supporting our teams, this was always challenging for me. How can we respond in a way that conveys genuine compassion for the person while also communicating that the person still has a responsibility to ensure the change is implemented? Over time, and after a few bumpy conversations, I found that there were five components to a successful conversation with a person feeling overwhelmed by the work:

1. Acknowledge change can be hard. Don't dismiss their feelings of being overwhelmed or that they "can't do this." These feelings are real, so treat them as such. Express understanding, demonstrate empathy, and let them know you care.

2. Remind them of the why and the purpose for the change effort. Revisit the reasons for the change, the best hopes for the change, and the data that helped us decide this change was critical for our school community. If you involved them in the decision-making process, reconnect them with the reasons they decided to support it in the first place. Be genuine, be specific, and be thorough.

3. Remind them of their value. Let them know you believe in them, that they are an essential member of the team, and that you can't do it without them. Share the confidence you have in them.

4. Offer support. Ask "How can I help?" "What do you need from me?" "Is there something we can take off your plate?" If they share something that you can do—do it! Commit! Follow through and make sure they have the support they need.

5. Thank them. Express your gratitude for their commitment, for their perseverance, for their willingness to push through the challenges to make school amazing for kids.

SYNAPSE

When a teacher seems overwhelmed, ask them "how can I help?" But make sure you're willing to help! It will be useful to jot down their needs and what you're doing to support them so that their request for help doesn't get unintentionally overlooked in the hustle and bustle.

Teacher	Need/Request	What I will do to help	Status (in progress/ complete)

Emotional intelligence isn't just the realm of sociologists and psychologists. It's important that as teacher supporters we understand what it is and how it can help both educators and students better understand themselves, their surroundings, and each other. The more educated we become about the nuances and the different types of emotions, the better we can regulate our emotional states and support teachers as they navigate their emotions.

As coaches, we can support teachers by affirming their emotions and partnering with them as we display emotional agility. By supporting teachers in emotional intelligence, teachers are better able to help students with managing their emotions. And being in touch with your emotions can better serve you and the relationships you have with your colleagues.

PATHWAY OF LEADERSHIP

LEADING EFFECTIVE TEAM MEETINGS

How often have you said to yourself, "I'm a coach, so that means I have to facilitate every team meeting or PLC meeting"? Actually, you don't have to, nor is that the best use of your time. Your role is to provide support and strategies to ensure there are structures for effective and productive team collaboration. In this section about the pathway of leadership, we will explore how to support your teacher-leaders, develop communication and collaboration structures, using decision-making supports, and creating an instructional coaching framework.

◆ IDENTIFY AND SUPPORT THE TEACHER-LEADER

Coaches frequently feel an obligation to facilitate every meeting. They feel they have to clone themselves to be able to be present for every single meeting while also juggling the many other activities they lead throughout the day. We know what happens when we try to keep too many plates spinning: we're not able to focus on priorities because too many things are vying for our attention. But there is another way, one that develops leadership capacity in teachers as well.

Coaches can best model collaboration when they're able to help build that capacity in others. Hello team leaders! You're not delegating just for the sake of it, you are empowering others to step into this role. When you do this, it means: 1) they own the process because they're personally invested and 2) your own capacity to support in more impactful ways is freed up. As a coach, your focus is to support the team leader as they orchestrate and facilitate the meeting. The teacher-leader will assist in decision-making and carrying out common agreements. They will create the team agendas and consult with the coach as needed. The team leader takes regular pulse checks and requests support from the coach to serve as a thought partner to create solutions and brainstorm ideas.

Team leaders should serve for one-year terms. This provides consistency for the year, without having to work through the challenge of a rotating facilitator, and it provides an opportunity for others to step into that. It's never too late to identify and empower a team leader.

◆ ESTABLISH A STRUCTURE FOR CONSISTENT COMMUNICATION

Your role can be best leveraged as a creator of structure. You have the opportunity to increase trust and transparency by creating safe and consistent outlets for communication. What kinds of topics will be discussed? Have norms been agreed upon by all? Who will send out the meeting action items and next steps? Even when you're working with team leaders, it's important that you, as the coach, model collaborative best practices during a meeting. It's important that you communicate the purpose of a team meeting: engaging teachers in a collective practice.

◆ ESTABLISH A TIMELINE

During collaborative team meetings, ideas and corresponding actions will emerge. Often, though, once we leave the meeting, we dive back into the hustle of planning and teaching, and sometimes those great ideas get lost in the shuffle. As coaches, we can help the team refocus on our collective goals. We can also help with establishing timelines for the work and emerging with ideas and corresponding actions. This isn't because we want compliance but because we want to ensure we're able to support with the resources and time to accomplish these goals that we've deemed important.

◆ CREATE A REPOSITORY

As coaches, we have a unique perspective on all the activities and initiatives occurring in the building as well as the everyday activities occurring in classrooms. Because of this comprehensive perspective, coaches are better able to curate and collect resources that may be helpful to many people in the building. The third-grade teacher that has been working on creating processes for student feedback may be of help to the fifth-grade teacher looking for similar supports for her classroom. As coaches, we get to make those mutually beneficial connections and start to create repositories of helpful tools, artifacts, protocols, and processes.

◆ PROVIDE FEEDBACK

We focus a lot of our feedback mechanisms on templates or tools that are used to aid in teaching and learning. We also focus on feedback for classroom observations and walkthroughs. But rarely do we focus feedback on how we're collaborating.

If you ask teachers what they wish would change about their circumstances, you'll get lots of comments about the desire for meetings to change. We can support high-quality collaborative environments by providing feedback to team leaders regarding collaborative practices used during a meeting.

When meeting with the team leader, these questions can help direct the conversation:

- What are some highlights from the meetings?
- What are some opportunities we've uncovered together?
- What are your roadblocks?
- What is something risky we've tried together as a team?
- How have you pushed others' thinking?

Now that you've created a purposeful plan for communication, let's discuss where this plan unfolds in the scope of the coach's day.

WHERE COACHING HAPPENS

Don't coach from the poop deck. Say what now? Okay, so now that I have your attention, a poop deck is formed from the roof of a cabin built in the rear of a ship. The name comes from the French word for a ship's stern, *la poupe*, from the Latin *puppis*. At the stern, the poop deck provides an elevated position ideal for observation. Similarly, we often coach from our office or "from above" because we have a fear of somehow looking inferior or less powerful. Ever heard the term *impostor syndrome*? It's the same idea. And it can affect the way you coach.

In the coaching world, could the poop deck be the coach's office? But that's where team meetings are held and where I conduct small-group professional development. I'm not just sitting in my office, I'm also busy with teams there. Could my elevated vantage point be the classroom? But shouldn't coaches be out in classrooms? I'm busy there with walkthroughs and engaging teachers in the coaching cycle. Yes, coaches should have an elevated view for observation. Coaches must have all relevant data and information to make the most informed decisions. Well, if it's not the office or the classroom, where is it? Really the poop deck isn't a place in the school building, but a metaphor for how our coaching role intersects with teaching and learning.

In the two examples I provided, I intentionally used the word *busy*. Additionally, I framed busy as a result of something that just happens—"I am busy because I'm a coach and there are many things to do and many demands placed on me." Here's the truth, though: being busy is a decision. I know, when you're going through a stressful period, it definitely doesn't feel like a choice. But you decide what you want to do and the things that are important to you. Even in situations where you don't feel like you have a lot of control, you actually do. You get to decide how you will tackle certain tasks, who you will interact with, and how your interactions will be carried out. You get to say yes or no. Think about the most important parts of your life: Your health and your family. We don't find the time to do things for our health or our family; we make the time to do things. If you aren't doing something because you're too busy, it's likely because the activity is not a priority for you.

So much of what we do in education is tied to being productive. We have checklists, unit plans, smart goals, and action plans. These are all great tools to help us act on our priorities. But when the list starts to build, there is a temptation to shortcut the process, and we do this by turning these items into to-do lists instead of opportunities to engage at a deeper level. When we start doing this day by day, we start coasting along without thinking.

An effective way of tackling "busyness" is by thinking through the parts of the day you have control over. For example: You've gotten up early, maybe you've exercised and had a cup of coffee or tea, and you're thinking about your day. You note that you have two PLC meetings to attend, have agreed to observe a classroom as a part of the coaching cycle, and will be facilitating an afternoon PD session. Those are events that are happening, and you probably don't have much control about whether they occur. What you can control is *how* you will engage in those activities. Ask yourself some questions as you approach these events:

PLC/team Meetings:

- What goals have been established for these?
- If I'm currently facilitating these, is there a plan to identify a team leader that can consistently facilitate meetings?
- If a team leader is facilitating these, how can I best support the team?
- How effective/productive are the team meetings? How do I know?
- Do team members feel like they each have shared ownership in the work that's happening in these meetings? How do I know? If not, how do I address?

The Coaching Cycle:

- Have I cultivated an authentic relationship with this teacher?
- In what ways can I establish a deeper trust with this teacher?
- Have I communicated my intentions with the teacher about my role in observing or modeling in her classroom?
- Does the teacher have a way to access prior conversations we've had?
- How can I make our past notes and discussions more accessible?
- Have I thought about my posture in the classroom and its potential perceptions?
- Do I know the needs of the classroom?

Professional Development:

- Have I sought input on the goals of this PD/training?
- Do teachers have a choice in the kinds of PD they attend?
- Have I provided differentiated activities in the PD to better meet the needs of teachers?
- How will I know if the PD was successful?
- How am I monitoring the success of PDs over the long haul?
- Do I ask other teachers to facilitate PDs as well?
- Have I ensured active learning in this PD, or does it risk becoming an information-dissemination session?
- Have I considered technology integration / blended learning for this PD?

These questions are written with purpose and intentionality. Even engaging in purpose and intentionality takes careful reflection. If you're not sure about where to start with reflection, use this simple T-chart (I've filled it in with an example of a coach reflecting on journaling).

What did you learn?	*What value does it have?*
I learned that journaling is valuable. As I think about my day, I feel that many of the activities and tasks I busy myself with on a daily basis don't have strong roots in my purpose as an educator. Many days, the urgent gets taken care of and those things are loosely connected to the most important goals and I allow "busyness" to get in the way of important work.	Most people would agree that journaling is a good thing but often let it reside as an inspirational statement instead of using it to reflect on the day. Journaling has helped me paint a clearer picture of my purpose and has allowed me to be more intentional with my day.

Many times, we go through our days checking off things that we "completed" but without truly knowing their impact. If we view our day as a bunch of tasks to check off, we're only concerned with the completion of the task and not fully engaging in the opportunity ahead of us. The kind of person, educator, and coach we are, and who we become, consists of the everyday things we do—not only what we do, but how we do them. Will we approach our tasks with purpose, intentionality, empathy, kindness, and courage, or will we approach them as just another busy day?

◆ WHAT DOES IT MEAN TO BE AN EXPERT?

We all started off as teachers, probably focused on a particular grade level or subject. But now that we're coaches, we worry about things like how to give feedback to the algebra teacher: "I never taught math, I only taught seventh-grade social studies, so how do I add value for that teacher?" Most of us as leaders and coaches have had these thoughts. This is a very real fear that we feel when we step into coaching roles. It's that fear of being exposed, the fear of people finding out that we aren't experts at everything having to do with teaching and learning that is called impostor syndrome. You may have heard that it applied to anyone who is struggling with self-doubt or having difficulty recognizing and owning their successes.

I think it's important to address this fear head-on. I ask coaches to reflect on what makes coaching hard, what gets in their way, and what they're afraid of. The fear of thinking they need to be an expert or they can't offer anything beneficial is widespread, so I tackle it head on. In my teaching career, I taught upper-level science courses—chemistry and physics. I've never been a kindergarten teacher, nor have I ever taught AP Spanish. Yet, I know I can add extreme value when I'm coaching a teacher of any subject in any grade level. And it's not because I've spent years deeply learning every single content area standard that needs to be taught in the K–12 curriculum. That would be unreasonable and unnecessary.

I do know, though, that I can observe a teacher teaching a content area or grade level that I have not taught and still have a lot to offer in a coaching conversation. Why is that? Because I have had coaches who were former elementary teachers and they gave me excellent feedback when I was a high school chemistry teacher. It's also because I take very seriously that the expertise I need to continually develop as a coach is a deep knowledge of exceptional pedagogy. I'm an expert at good teaching. I learn about it, read about it, talk about it, engage with it, study it in a variety of ways. And I have been doing that for years. So, while I might not be an expert at the content being taught at a deep level, I will understand the pedagogical moves being made to teach it, and that's how I add value. You do the exact same thing, and you add unique value based on your varied experiences.

In fact, admitting that you aren't an expert in everything can actually help break down barriers and make coaching more of the partnership you are hoping it will be. One of my favorite ways to start a coaching conversation with a teacher is by saying something like, "I always learn so much about this content area when I'm in your classroom watching you teach. I'd love for you to share with me where today's lesson fits into the big picture. What are you hoping your students will know and be able to do?" I love hearing teachers talk about their content and letting them know that they are teaching me, too. It also gives me insights into their teaching moves, which can help me be a better coach.

Free yourself from the idea that you have to be the expert in everything. You don't, and if you try, you will only fail miserably. If you are a literacy coach, you of course need to be strong in your understanding of reading and writing. If you're a math coach, you absolutely need to have content expertise in mathematics. But many of us serve in roles where we are expected to coach multiple grade levels and content areas. If you want to increase your confidence and competence as a coach, become an ongoing student of impactful pedagogy. Continue to hone your expertise in how to teach in ways that dramatically increase student learning, and you will always have something of value to bring to the table. As I moved into leadership roles, I also made sure to be a student of what good leadership and coaching looks like, so that, as a principal and coach, I was able to add value no matter the circumstances or situation of the school.

HELPING OTHERS BE THEIR MOST CREATIVES SELVES THROUGH PURPOSEFUL DECISION-MAKING

You know that feeling when you're collaborating, and, after a bit, you finally find the creative zone. At the beginning of the meeting there weren't many ideas being generated, and then all of a sudden, ideas are exploding from the group. Ideas are flowing, and team members feel confident about making decisions. You might think this elusive feeling of being "in the zone" just happens, but actually, you can create the conditions for these creative explosions.

One of the biggest factors in creating these circumstances is the freedom and autonomy to make decisions—and make them with confidence—even if you don't think you have the perfect conditions or every piece of information. We call these reversible decisions. Reversible decisions are the Google Docs of decisions. They can be edited after the fact, and even restored from a previous. Irreversible decisions are the PDFs of decisions—final. Once you save a document as a PDF, it's very difficult to change it. Reversible decisions can be made quickly, and irreversible decisions require deliberate consideration.

Some examples of reversible decisions include:

- Goals for a coaching cycle
- PLC meeting frequency
- The topic for a professional development session you're facilitating
- What professional book you're reading
- A new student-engagement strategy

Some examples of irreversible decisions are:

- How you respond to a teacher asking for help
- Who you hire for your team
- Your level of engagement with teachers
- Your level of engagement with the principal
- Your level of engagement with students and parents

It could be argued that every decision is reversible. Yes, of course, in a way. It's never too late to change course when you see another way. But the point is some decisions have a tremendous impact, certain rewards, and consequences. Wouldn't it be helpful to have a more thoughtful approach to decision-making?

A decision journal can be very helpful. When you've made a decision, write it down, describe it, and record what you believe its impact will be. The decision journal can be a record of all your previous decisions. It allows you to analyze the decisions you've made without getting caught in the typical trap of cognitive justification in retrospect.

Many times, when a negative outcome resulting from a previous decision occurs, we explain it and even justify it on other related patterns and then create a predictable excuse for it. Think about a new initiative or program that you implemented that just flopped. After it flopped, maybe you tried to explain it and concluded that a lack of fidelity to a consistent and sound framework explained why the program was unsuccessful. Or maybe you concluded that there wasn't an ongoing support structure of professional development, which allowed the plan to fizzle. Therein lies the fragility in our reflective processes: we think that we've created a sturdy plan only to change the narrative when an unexpected event occurs. A decision journal allows you to predict outcomes right after you make a decision and then compare the prediction to what actually happens. This practice also contributes to a leader being willing to admit mistakes and think about future growth areas. Farnam Street (2021), a mental-models group, created a decision template that can be a helpful starting place.

Decision No.:

Date:

Time:

Decision:

Mental/Physical State:

☐ Energized	☐ Focused	☐ Relaxed
☐ Confident	☐ Tired	☐ Accepting
☐ Accommodating	☐ Anxious	☐ Resigned
☐ Frustrated	☐ Angry	

The situation/context:

The problem statement or frame:

The variables that govern the situation include:

The complications/complexities as I see them:

Alternatives that were seriously considered and not chosen were:

Explain the range of outcomes:

What I expect to happen and the actual probabilities are:

The outcome:

Review Date (six months after decision date):

What happened and what I learned:

Example:

Decision No.: 6

Date: January 10, 2021

Time: 9:00 a.m.

Decision: Having a conversation with a resistant teacher

Mental/Physical State:

☑ Energized	☑ Focused	☐ Relaxed
☐ Confident	☐ Tired	☐ Accepting
☐ Accommodating	☑ Anxious	☐ Resigned
☐ Frustrated	☐ Angry	

The situation/context:
The last time I presented some instructional math strategies to our K–6 team, there was a teacher that provided some harsh criticism on the feedback form. This is a teacher that is regularly negative and resistant to any new strategies. This time, in her feedback, she critiqued me personally as a coach, saying that I have never taught her grade level and what would I know about teaching her students.

The problem statement or frame:
Ms. Jones is resisting any new strategies that I share with her, which will have a negative effect on student learning and growth and in her own growth as a teacher. It also puts a barrier up for future collaboration and dialogue.

The variables that govern the situation include:
The relationship I have with Ms. Jones.
Her attitude.
My attitude toward her and the situation.
The culture in the building.

The complications/complexities as I see them:
As I see things, Ms. Jones has an aversion toward me because she feels stressed and frustrated.

Alternatives that were seriously considered and not chosen were:
Ignore Ms. Jones and not confront her.

Explain the range of outcomes:
Ms. Jones could become angry and more resistant.
Ms. Jones could become apathetic and just not engage.
Ms. Jones could eventually become an ally.

What I expect to happen and the actual probabilities are:
After I have a conversation with her, affirm her expertise, and allow her to
vent her frustrations, over time I think she will change her posture toward me
and become more open to suggestions. I think she could eventually become
my ally.

The outcome:
She was very quiet and distant during the beginning of our conversation,
but once I opened up about some of my own fears and frustrations, she
began to open up about hers. We ended the meeting on a productive tone.

Review Date (six months after decision date): July 10, 2021

What happened and what I learned:
Six months later, Ms. Jones has been much more open about trying new
strategies. She is still very brash and opinionated, but now that we've come
to an understanding, I'm able to use her feedback constructively.

Highlighting past decisions and making connections to our current reality can provide a powerful context for new ideas and creativity. It allows us, as leaders, to accept the unpredictable nature of education and the world we live in, and we learn to adapt to this truth by taking risks and thinking in new ways. The decisions we make can have a lasting impact, and improving the process of decision-making and reflection can push our practices even further.

◆ GOING BEYOND "PLANNING TIME"

I was an administrator of a school that had just been declared a STEM magnet school. The immediate response to STEM is often a quick inclusion of hands-on activities. These out-of-the-box explorations provide easy access to materials, hands-on experiences, and lots of teacher support. But we couldn't stop there. That wasn't STEM. We had to rethink how were planning and how we were designing learning experiences. If we were going to move toward more student inquiry and creativity, we had to move toward more teacher inquiry and creativity as well.

How would we create collaborative structures for teachers to co-create student-centric, problem-based challenges? I knew we needed a "defined autonomy" model, a space where we could implement reversible decisions but with predefined boundaries. An example of this was that, as a school, we decided that we would all stick with the district-recommended math scope and sequence, but we would have completely free rein on the science scope and sequence. If it made more sense to pull a science concept from March and teach it in September, we would have at it. We knew that it was important to have a learning progression for math, but that a science pacing guide was not necessarily ordered the same way (because it's more conceptual and less contingent on skill building). Once we established this new rule, teachers found so much more freedom to develop STEM projects and challenges without being hindered by static scope and sequences.

Planning for rigorous and relevant teaching and learning requires more than just "common planning time." It represents a consistent, purposeful, and protected time where teachers immerse themselves in collaborative environments for the sole purpose of collectively creating integrated challenges and scaffolded lessons. Teachers' time is extremely valuable, and therefore we must ensure collaborative planning doesn't become another compliance-driven activity. Often, highly effective and passionate teachers jump in over their heads, and a disproportionate amount of actions and products are generated by those same teachers.

Our new way of collaboration opened up a more innovative approach to teaching and learning in our newly defined STEM blocks. STEM projects and challenges that were planned were going to be facilitated during these STEM blocks. Every day would look different, and so planning would become very important. Teachers and administrators embraced flexibility in differentiation via small-group instruction during student-directed challenge time or planned to devote a block of time to teaching a mini math lesson while relating it back to the challenge's essential question, which had roots in the science context. Differentiated student voice and choice promoted opportunities for students to choose their own pathways to a solution. If teachers spotted deficits, they would use them as impromptu learning opportunities to differentiate inside of this challenge-based environment. During a one-hour meeting, you would see high fives, goals agreed upon and discussed, action-oriented strategies and tactics shared, and artifacts being produced.

You might have expected this chapter to be more focused on attitudes about creativity or wide-scale structural changes to help dismantle our current school culture in favor of collaborative brainstorming sessions and "genius hour" time for teachers every day. At this point in our current culture, that's not something we often currently have the luxury of doing. Our schools are underfunded and lack resources and time, so we must change the way we approach our everyday choices and decisions. By incorporating a mindful and intentional approach to decision-making, we're able to better implement creative ideas and analyze their effectiveness.

BUILDING AN INSTRUCTIONAL COACHING FRAMEWORK

The instructional coaching framework is a map of sorts, and it's just one crucial part of the larger system of pathways in the coaching connectome. So why develop an instructional coaching framework? While reading this book, maybe you have put together a plan for how you will partner with teachers or lead change in your school building. This is fantastic, but everyone must be on the same page for these coaching strategies to be effective. Everyone must know their role in relation to your role as the coach. Before we can develop an instructional coaching framework, we have to agree as a team on goals or collective commitments that we are going to hold each other accountable for. We call these collective agreements.

Here are some examples of collective agreements a team might decide on:

• We will provide students with multiple opportunities to demonstrate their thinking and learning.
• We will discuss the best instructional strategies and evaluate their impact on student learning.
• We will integrate social-emotional-learning competencies in our unit/lesson planning.
• We will create a collaborative structure to ensure our PBL projects are relevant, meaningful, and aligned to standards.

After we decide on our collective agreements, we then decide what role we will each play in ensuring we're able to best meet these agreements.

First, decide what the role of the coach, district, and building will be. Below are examples of what these roles could look like:

The Role of the Coach

The role of the coach is to empower and support teachers in a way that positively impacts student learning.

The Role of the District

The role of the district is to communicate agreed-upon and shared instructional priorities and provide resources to schools to ensure priorities are supported.

The Role of the Building Administration and Staff

The role of the building administration and staff is to develop a positive culture that supports innovative teaching practices and positive student-learning experiences.

After the roles are agreed upon, it's time to design an instructional framework. Before you start, consider this analogy: Think of the elements that make up the framework of your home. The wall framing, plumbing, electrical system, and drywall are all important elements for a safe and well-functioning home. You can move furniture around, change out light fixtures, or freshen up a room with paint, but the foundational elements are constant. The same is true for an instructional coaching framework: Your agreed-upon roles and actions will stay consistent throughout the year unless the school/district vision/mission changes. It's important to know how each person will support these collective agreements.

Below is an example of an outline of an instructional coaching framework:

◆ THE ROLE OF THE COACH

- Coaches create a culture of trust and transparency with teachers and staff.

- The coach functions as a catalyst for change, cultivating divergent thinking and a culture of inquiry in the school building.
- The coach will create authentic and meaningful professional learning experiences for teachers and staff.
- The coach acts as a partner who learns alongside the teacher and the principal.
- The coach will facilitate coaching cycles to ensure collective agreements are aligned to the school vision and are a part of daily practice.
- The coach will engage in their own professional learning by reading relevant research and attending professional development aligned to best coaching and teaching practices.
- Coaches and building administrators will have a regular cadence to review challenges and goals, and discuss trends they are observing.

◆ THE ROLE OF THE PRINCIPAL

- The principal will facilitate the creation of a school vision, gathering input from all stakeholders in the process.
- The principal will clarify and communicate the role of the coach to all stakeholders.
- The principal will ensure the implementation of collective agreements.
- The principal will model best leadership practices, consistently and frequently communicate information, collect input, create processes and structures, and ensure collaboration among all stakeholders.
- The principal will engage in their own professional learning by reading relevant research and attending professional development aligned to best leadership and teaching practices.
- The principal will ensure the creation of processes to promote efficiences, communicating purpose, creating buy-in, and ensuring each educator has a part to play.

◆ *THE ROLE OF THE TEACHERS*

- The teacher will engage in their own professional learning by reading relevant research and attending professional development aligned to best teaching practices.
- The teachers will actively seek to reflect upon and implement professional development, asking questions and providing feedback along the way.
- The teachers will partner with coaches in the development of a coaching cycle that is aligned with agreed-upon goals.
- The teachers will actively engage in collaborative team planning, serving as PLC/team leaders and using data to inform strategies and next steps.

◆ *THE ROLE OF THE DISTRICT*

- The district will consistently and frequently communicate information, collect input, create processes and structures, and ensure collaboration among all stakeholders.
- The district will provide leadership around the development of an instructional coaching framework.
- The district will ensure the instructional coaching framework is posted after the collaborative process of development is completed.
- The district will provide leadership around the development of a district vision for teaching and learning.
- The district will create and/or provide access to instructional resources, and on-demand instructional support.
- The district will support coaches in their professional learning with external and internal PD opportunities.

It's important that you go through the process and develop this framework with your teams. I have provided a guide and some examples to support your work, but full ownership will only happen if each person on the team provides input and is actively a part of the process.

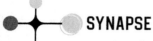

SYNAPSE

Create and implement your instructional coaching framework:

1. Start with your school vision (this might need to be refined or re-created if it hasn't been revisited in a while).

2. Create your common agreements, the goals and commitments that are decided upon collectively as a team.

3. Next, define the role of each stakeholder the coach supports and partners with.

4. Once you've created your common agreements, you're ready to build your instructional framework. Your framework defines the roles in relation to your common agreements, which are aligned to the school vision.

5. After you've created your framework, provide an opportunity for all to ask questions and to provide feedback.

To be at our most efficient and productive, we need to be able to switch back and forth between following the framework and then having an open discussion of what's working and what's not. A framework is just a structure, a support, and agreed-upon principles, but it's not meant to be the be-all and end-all. Sometimes we really need to step back and contemplate the wider view.

This is particularly true for educators. We frequently get stuck in the habit of reacting to events on an hour-by-hour basis so we almost completely lose the focus of what our role is and how we can best support teachers. Use this framework as a guide, but never be afraid to step back into the open position to consider new evidence and new approaches.

It's important for you to ensure that teachers have a voice in what support looks like from you. Asking about this is a strategy for clarifying roles and expectations, and it helps set the vision for the instructional coaching framework. Teachers will feel like they're not being valued or heard when they feel like they aren't getting the support they need. Asking about their hopes for support up front helps teachers be actively involved in thinking about what type of support would be helpful, and it holds them accountable for asking for what they need. The strategies and framework included in this section promote everyone sharing input and create psychological safety for everyone to engage at the highest levels and be their most creative selves.

EPILOGUE

In this book, I have used my own experiences to share with you the intricacies of coaching, its impact, its traps, its rewards, and what we can do to optimize ourselves for everything involved in it. Instructional coaching is so much more than actions and behaviors—"This teacher needs support, so I'll do this," or "The school has that PD need, so I'll facilitate an after-school session." The way we collaborate with teachers affects how we're perceived when facilitating professional development, which affects our leadership, which impacts the school culture, which affects the decisions we make. In order for actions to have a transformative impact, they must be tied to goals and goals tied to a vision. In this book we've seen how all these pathways are interconnected to one another: the instructional coaching connection.

As you look at the connection as a whole, important pathways with connective touch points emerge. Coaches should reflect on their purpose and what makes them passionate. This passion is visibly exuded in their work with teachers. Increased and consistent visibility work to create a culture of rapport. As coaches build this rapport, they see evidence of their own confidence building and this leads to teachers feeling confident in the support they're receiving. Relationships are embraced as a process and not forced as a means to an end. Relationships are nurtured through awareness of language used, with effective feedback that balances positive and critical responses, a resistance to compliance culture, and the aim of incorporating a mix of collaboration and independence. As coaches go about their daily work, they show empathy and learn to listen actively, and they employ self-care so they stay connected to what gives them enthusiasm. As coaches are communicating, leading, and collaborating, they should be developing a sense of emotional intelligence, agility, and capability in empowering others. They should work to help others feel more creative and institute a process for a shared instructional coaching framework that clearly outlines everyone's role in the process.

I'd like to conclude with a few thoughts about other important elements for preparing for successful coaching.

◆ POSTURE

If you're continually feeling like you're controlled by your to-do lists, putting out fires, and reacting to problems, then it will be very difficult to be or feel like an effective coach. Working under pressure will never allow you to feel creative, collaborative, or present in your role as a coach. You might not be able to control everything hurled at you, but you can control how you respond. You have complete control of your approach and can hold a posture of confidence, strength, perseverance, and calm. Take a first step, even if that means just taking a deep breath.

◆ HUMOR

Smiles impact our interactions with others and our life experience as social beings. Smiles and laughter create an inviting tone, an essential warmth, and students learn best in welcoming environments of inclusivity. Teachers also collaborate and work more effectively in these environments. Humor activates the brain's dopamine reward system. Finding humor in the everyday is not only a tool for a more fulfilling life, but a powerful act of creativity for teachers and students.

Those who find the "small joys" in everyday moments of life smile often and laugh frequently. If you're having trouble finding bright spots, just look around and be present. Find a bird, a cloud, or a tree, or simply take two minutes, walk away from your desk, and look up at the sky. There's always something somewhere that has the power to give us the gift of joy, as long as we are open and present to experience it. You will begin to find the nuances of the everyday. Gradually, and without even being conscious of it, you will start to notice the many small wonders surrounding you.

◆ BOUNDARIES

To do anything meaningful, you must create the space to set yourself up for success. As coaches we give, give, give, and give. At times it feels like everyone needs us all the time. Every writer needs to carve out hours in the day to write and create a physical space around them that enables them to create their best work. Educators have to do this as well. Often, we might think, "Oh, if I had more office time I could plan better professional development," or "If I didn't have to respond to so many emails I'd have more time to be in classrooms." The good news is that you get to draw your own boundaries. You get to create that space that makes you successful. Set boundaries on your time. Instead of spreading yourself thin, or sprinkling your help and support 24/7, take a "burst" approach: Do it all in a short amount of time and carve out a burst of help. This approach will also result in a higher mood and more focused energy. You'll feel you made a difference and can focus on yourself and your to-do items in other planned blocks.

◆ FOCUS

Focus is contingent on setting boundaries. Once you've created that space in your world, you're able to dedicate time to focusing your energies. It might be a new, innovative instructional strategy or maybe it's thinking through how you're going to work with a resistant teacher—both require focused energy to develop a strategy and a plan. It also will cost time and comfort and require trial and error. That is okay. Anything worthwhile is going to take time and may cause temporary confusion.

◆ *COURAGE*

How do we find our courage? Well, we actually possess all the courage we would ever need. Sometimes we all need to be reminded of how brave we've already been thus far. We also have to continually act with bravery, doing the right thing and even the risky thing, even though we're scared, timid, or hesitant.

Do you know what takes courage? Asking for help. No one can do it all by themselves, and no one should ever think they're supposed to. Ask your colleagues for help. Don't facilitate that PD by yourself, enlist others to facilitate. Not only will it help you with your workload, it will demonstrate your willingness to be collaborative. When you ask for help, the helper also feels needed and affirmed. You trusted them enough to ask for help? You have confidence in their ability. Everyone wins! The signposts of courage in our school buildings and in our collaborative school environments are displayed in our willingness to take on conflict, welcome criticism, ask for help, establish complete transparency, cultivate healthy relationships, and communicate our purpose. I hope this book has helped you tap into the courage you already have and has provided you with resources and tools to boldly coach and create new pathways in your school.

Supporting teachers matters right now more than ever. There are so many things challenging teachers—a pandemic, social and political ill will toward educators, lack of funding, poor pay, competing priorities, etc. You can become a lighthouse for teachers in a swirling storm of stress and strife. You can make a difference in the lives of students, because you're a positive force of leadership and support for teachers. There is no single huge action or fix; it's the daily moments of you showing up, and you showing up as only you can that matter.

ACKNOWLEDGMENTS

The reason this book exists is because of the people listed here who believe in me and support me and my endeavors.

Herbie: For taking care of me, our boys, and our home so masterfully, and for your humor, genius, patience, and unconditional love.

Clayton: For your tenacity, independence, and strength.

Anna: For your kindness, courage, and heart.

Mom: For your love, care, and belief that I could do anything.

Dave: For your constancy, loyalty, and sagacity.

Jim Knight: For your vision, your wisdom, and the impact you've forever made on the world of coaching.

Shelley Burgess: For devoting your talent and passion to leadership and for making this book possible.

DBC Inc. crew: Dave and Shelley, Salvatore, and Laura.

REFERENCES

David, S. (2016). Emotional agility: get unstuck, embrace change, and thrive in work and life. London: Penguin Life.

Dweck, C. S. (2006). Mindset: the new psychology of success. New York: Random House.

Farnam Street. (2021). fs.blog.

Lang, N. (2018). Everyday instructional coaching: seven daily drivers to support teacher effectiveness. Solution Tree: Bloomington.

McRaney, D. (2013). You are now less dumb: how to conquer mob mentality, how to buy happiness, and all the other ways to outsmart yourself. New York: Avery.

Polman, E., & Emich, K. J. (2011). Decisions for others are more creative than decisions for the self. Personality and Social Psychology Bulletin, 37(4), 492–501.

Sagan, C. (1995). The demon-haunted world: science as a candle in the dark. New York: Random House.

Stutman, R. (2020). The essence of leadership: Randall Stutman on the knowledge project. Podcast notes. 14 Nov. 2020. Podcastnotes.org/ knowledge-project/randall-stutman-on-the-knowledge-project/.

ABOUT
NATHAN D. LANG-RAAD

Nathan D. Lang-Raad, EdD, is an international speaker, author, and educator. He is currently the vice president of strategy at Savvas, and he was previously the chief education officer at WeVideo. Throughout his career, he has served as a teacher, principal, university adjunct professor, consultant, and education strategist. He was director of elementary curriculum and instruction for Metropolitan Nashville Public Schools and the education supervisor at NASA's Johnson Space Center. He has also served as the president-elect of the ISTE Ed Leaders Professional Learning Network.

Nathan is the author of *Everyday Instructional Coaching*, co-author of *The New Art and Science of Teaching Mathematics* with Dr. Robert J. Marzano, author of *WeVideo Every Day*, co-author of *Mathematics Unit Planning in a PLC at Work, Grades PreK–2*, co-author of *The Teachers of Oz* with Herbie Raad, and co-author of the *Boundless Classroom* with Dr James V. Witty.

Nathan resides in the beautiful state of Maine with his husband, Herbie. To learn more about Nathan's work, visit drlangraad.com or follow him on Twitter and Instagram at @drlangraad.

MORE FROM

Since 2012, DBCI has published books that inspire and equip educators to be their best. For more information on our titles or to purchase bulk orders for your school, district, or book study, visit DaveBurgessConsulting.com/DBCIbooks.

Like a PIRATE™ Series

Teach Like a PIRATE by Dave Burgess
eXPlore Like a PIRATE by Michael Matera
Learn Like a PIRATE by Paul Solarz
Plan Like a PIRATE by Dawn M. Harris
Play Like a PIRATE by Quinn Rollins
Run Like a PIRATE by Adam Welcome
Tech Like a PIRATE by Matt Miller

Lead Like a PIRATE™ Series

Lead Like a PIRATE by Shelley Burgess and Beth Houf
Balance Like a PIRATE by Jessica Cabeen, Jessica Johnson, and Sarah Johnson
Lead beyond Your Title by Nili Bartley
Lead with Appreciation by Amber Teamann and Melinda Miller
Lead with Culture by Jay Billy
Lead with Instructional Rounds by Vicki Wilson
Lead with Literacy by Mandy Ellis
She Leads by Dr. Rachael George and Majalise W. Tolan

Leadership & School Culture

Beyond the Surface of Restorative Practices by Marisol Rerucha

Choosing to See by Pamela Seda and Kyndall Brown

Culturize by Jimmy Casas

Discipline Win by Andy Jacks

Escaping the School Leader's Dunk Tank by Rebecca Coda and
   Rick Jetter

Fight Song by Kim Bearden

From Teacher to Leader by Starr Sackstein

If the Dance Floor Is Empty, Change the Song by Joe Clark

The Innovator's Mindset by George Couros

It's OK to Say "They" by Christy Whittlesey

Kids Deserve It! by Todd Nesloney and Adam Welcome

Let Them Speak by Rebecca Coda and Rick Jetter

The Limitless School by Abe Hege and Adam Dovico

Live Your Excellence by Jimmy Casas

Next-Level Teaching by Jonathan Alsheimer

The Pepper Effect by Sean Gaillard

Principaled by Kate Barker, Kourtney Ferrua, and Rachael George

The Principled Principal by Jeffrey Zoul and Anthony McConnell

Relentless by Hamish Brewer

The Secret Solution by Todd Whitaker, Sam Miller, and Ryan Donlan

Start. Right. Now. by Todd Whitaker, Jeffrey Zoul, and Jimmy Casas

Stop. Right. Now. by Jimmy Casas and Jeffrey Zoul

Teachers Deserve It by Rae Hughart and Adam Welcome

Teach Your Class Off by CJ Reynolds

They Call Me "Mr. De" by Frank DeAngelis

Thrive through the Five by Jill M. Siler

Unmapped Potential by Julie Hasson and Missy Lennard

When Kids Lead by Todd Nesloney and Adam Dovico

Word Shift by Joy Kirr

Your School Rocks by Ryan McLane and Eric Lowe

Technology & Tools

50 Things to Go Further with Google Classroom by Alice Keeler and Libbi Miller

50 Things You Can Do with Google Classroom by Alice Keeler and Libbi Miller

140 Twitter Tips for Educators by Brad Currie, Billy Krakower, and Scott Rocco

Block Breaker by Brian Aspinall

Building Blocks for Tiny Techies by Jamila "Mia" Leonard

Code Breaker by Brian Aspinall

The Complete EdTech Coach by Katherine Goyette and Adam Juarez

Control Alt Achieve by Eric Curts

The Esports Education Playbook by Chris Aviles, Steve Isaacs, Christine Lion-Bailey, and Jesse Lubinsky

Google Apps for Littles by Christine Pinto and Alice Keeler

Master the Media by Julie Smith

Raising Digital Leaders by Jennifer Casa-Todd

Reality Bytes by Christine Lion-Bailey, Jesse Lubinsky, and Micah Shippee, PhD

Sail the 7 Cs with Microsoft Education by Becky Keene and Kathi Kersznowski

Shake Up Learning by Kasey Bell

Social LEADia by Jennifer Casa-Todd

Stepping Up to Google Classroom by Alice Keeler and Kimberly Mattina

Teaching Math with Google Apps by Alice Keeler and Diana Herrington

Teachingland by Amanda Fox and Mary Ellen Weeks

Teaching with Google Jamboard by Alice Keeler and Kimberly Mattina

Teaching Methods & Materials

All 4s and 5s by Andrew Sharos

Boredom Busters by Katie Powell

The Classroom Chef by John Stevens and Matt Vaudrey

The Collaborative Classroom by Trevor Muir

Copyrighteous by Diana Gill

CREATE by Bethany J. Petty

Ditch That Homework by Matt Miller and Alice Keeler

Ditch That Textbook by Matt Miller

Don't Ditch That Tech by Matt Miller, Nate Ridgway, and Angelia Ridgway

EDrenaline Rush by John Meehan

Educated by Design by Michael Cohen, The Tech Rabbi

The EduProtocol Field Guide by Marlena Hebern and Jon Corippo

The EduProtocol Field Guide: Book 2 by Marlena Hebern and Jon Corippo

The EduProtocol Field Guide: Math Edition by Lisa Nowakowski and Jeremiah Ruesch

Expedition Science by Becky Schnekser

Frustration Busters by Katie Powell

Fully Engaged by Michael Matera and John Meehan

Game On? Brain On! by Lindsay Portnoy, PhD

Guided Math AMPED by Reagan Tunstall

Innovating Play by Jessica LaBar-Twomy and Christine Pinto

Instant Relevance by Denis Sheeran

Keeping the Wonder by Jenna Copper, Ashley Bible, Abby Gross, and Staci Lamb

LAUNCH by John Spencer and A.J. Juliani

Make Learning MAGICAL by Tisha Richmond

Pass the Baton by Kathryn Finch and Theresa Hoover

Project-Based Learning Anywhere by Lori Elliott

Pure Genius by Don Wettrick

The Revolution by Darren Ellwein and Derek McCoy

Shift This! by Joy Kirr

Skyrocket Your Teacher Coaching by Michael Cary Sonbert

Spark Learning by Ramsey Musallam

Sparks in the Dark by Travis Crowder and Todd Nesloney

Table Talk Math by John Stevens

Unpack Your Impact by Naomi O'Brien and LaNesha Tabb

The Wild Card by Hope and Wade King

The Writing on the Classroom Wall by Steve Wyborney

You Are Poetry by Mike Johnston

Inspiration, Professional Growth & Personal Development

Be REAL by Tara Martin

Be the One for Kids by Ryan Sheehy

The Coach ADVenture by Amy Illingworth

Creatively Productive by Lisa Johnson

Educational Eye Exam by Alicia Ray

The EduNinja Mindset by Jennifer Burdis

Empower Our Girls by Lynmara Colón and Adam Welcome

Finding Lifelines by Andrew Grieve and Andrew Sharos

The Four O'Clock Faculty by Rich Czyz

How Much Water Do We Have? by Pete and Kris Nunweiler

P Is for Pirate by Dave and Shelley Burgess

A Passion for Kindness by Tamara Letter

The Path to Serendipity by Allyson Apsey

Rogue Leader by Rich Czyz

Sanctuaries by Dan Tricarico

Saving Sycamore by Molly B. Hudgens

The SECRET SAUCE by Rich Czyz

Shattering the Perfect Teacher Myth by Aaron Hogan

Stories from Webb by Todd Nesloney

Talk to Me by Kim Bearden

Teach Better by Chad Ostrowski, Tiffany Ott, Rae Hughart, and Jeff Gargas

Teach Me, Teacher by Jacob Chastain

Teach, Play, Learn! by Adam Peterson

The Teachers of Oz by Herbie Raad and Nathan Lang-Raad

TeamMakers by Laura Robb and Evan Robb

Through the Lens of Serendipity by Allyson Apsey

The Zen Teacher by Dan Tricarico

Children's Books

Beyond Us by Aaron Polansky

Cannonball In by Tara Martin

Dolphins in Trees by Aaron Polansky

I Can Achieve Anything by MoNique Waters

I Want to Be a Lot by Ashley Savage

The Princes of Serendip by Allyson Apsey

Ride with Emilio by Richard Nares

The Wild Card Kids by Hope and Wade King

Zom-Be a Design Thinker by Amanda Fox

Printed in Great Britain
by Amazon